No Strangers Here

A Simplified Guide to Travel in Newfoundland

1997 Edition

Arthur M. Sullivan

No Strangers Here

A Simplified Guide to Travel in Newfoundland

1997 Edition

Arthur M. Sullivan

Creative Publishers
St. John's, Newfoundland
1995

∝ Printed on acid-free paper

Cover: Sylvia Ficken

Published by
CREATIVE BOOK PUBLISHING
A Division of 10699 Newfoundland Limited
A Robinson-Blackmore Printing & Publishing associated company
P.O. Box 8660, St. John's, Newfoundland A1B 3T7

First Edition, June 1995
Second Edition, May 1997

Printed in Canada by:
ROBINSON-BLACKMORE PRINTING & PUBLISHING

Canadian Cataloguing in Publication Data

Arthur M. Sullivan, 1932–

No strangers here

ISBN 1-895387-54-X

1. Newfoundland — Guidebooks. 2. Folklore — Newfoundland
I. Title.

FC2157.S85 1995   917.1804'4   C95-950152-5
F1122.S85 1995

To my parents:
Rose M. Sullivan ,
who by lesson and example first instilled in me
an appreciation of the wonder and beauty of
outport Newfoundland,
and
William (Bill) Sullivan
— long-term store clerk at Ryan Brothers —
who exemplified every one of the positive characteristics
which made outport Newfoundlanders a special breed.
And to my Granddaughter Mary Ann,
who, at five years, shows definite signs of developing
the same love of Newfoundland
shared by her great grandparents,
her grandparents and her parents.

ACKNOWLEDGEMENTS

Many people have rendered valuable assistance in the preparation of this volume. My son David contributed important background research and helpful suggestions. My daughter, Joan, edited the manuscript with her usual style. Marilyn Butland of the Department of Tourism, Culture and Recreation arranged for permission for the sections of *Historic Newfoundland* to be included. Marilyn Hicks typed the manuscript several times with great patience and expertise. Valerie Rowe prepared the maps with speed, efficiency and flair. Bernice St. Croix read the manuscript with a judicial and critical eye and a fierce loyalty to Central Newfoundland. Shannie Duff also read the manuscript with her usual careful scrutiny, and made helpful suggestions. Also the Cupids Historical Society provided helpful criticism.And, of course, Don Morgan of Creative Publishers was supportive and innovative throughout. To all these and to the numerous others who helped in various ways, I extend my sincere and heartfelt thanks.

TABLE OF CONTENTS

PREFACE TO SECOND EDITION

This is the second edition of *No Strangers Here*. The first edition was well received and in fact sold out. The basic format of this guide has not been changed, but some errors have been corrected, a chapter on exploring Newfoundland by sea has been added, and the sections on attractions and accommodations has been expanded and updated. I hope that this guide continues to be helpful to local travellers and visitors alike.

INTRODUCTION to the FIRST EDITION

It has been my very good fortune to have had the opportunity over the past 30 years to travel to various parts of the province under the most favourable of circumstances.

I was born and raised in Trinity, Trinity Bay, and, after completing high school there, spent most of my academic career as a student and later a professor at Memorial University in St. John's. During this time I became very familiar with the east coast of the island. My two years as Principal of the Grenfell College in Corner Brook gave me a knowledge of, and sincere appreciation for, the west coast and southern Labrador. My five years as Director of the Memorial University's Extension Service and my appointment as chief commissioner of the Commission of Inquiry into Newfoundland Transportation provided me with a close and unique view of the remainder of the province, as well as renewing my knowledge of those parts that I was already familiar with. Wherever I travelled, friends and colleagues who were intimately familiar with areas which I was to visit, often introduced me to the best (often less well known) restaurants and bed and breakfast establishments.

Years ago, friends and acquaintances who planned to travel to places or regions in Newfoundland began to ask my advice — which I was always glad to provide. Eventually the number of requests became so great that I gathered my advice together in a little booklet titled *Off the Beaten Track*. The booklet is no longer available, and in recent years new attractions and establishments have appeared. Recently, as I was trying to decide whether I would publish a revision of the brochure, I became aware that a very valuable and popular booklet of the Department of Tourism, *Historic Newfoundland*, was out of print and would not be republished. Accordingly, I asked the Newfoundland Department of Tourism and Culture for permission to reprint sections of that booklet, and this was rapidly and generously given.

This present publication is, therefore, a combination of a revision of my earlier efforts plus major sections from *Historic Newfoundland*.

(The sections which appeared originally in *Historic Newfoundland* are so identified.)

How To Use This Guide

This publication, like my previous one, is a simplified and specialized guide to travelling in Newfoundland. It is a highly personal presentation of information and a series of recommendations which I hope will meet with your approval and make your visit to Newfoundland more enjoyable and educational. The primary audience for whom this boot is intended is individuals travelling in their own cars and thus free to select their own routes and destinations. It is expected that this group will obtain maximum benefit from these pages although individuals travelling on tours or by public transportation may also find much of the material interesting and helpful.

Unlike many travel guidebooks this is not intended to be a detailed account of all aspects of travel in Newfoundland, but is a careful selection of information, some of which is highly personal and evaluative. For those who wish to have publications which are more comprehensive and impersonal many excellent ones are available free of charge from the Department of Tourism and Culture. Local development associations and tourist committees have also produced colourful and attractive descriptions of specific areas. Virtually all are first-rate and informative and I recommend them without reservation. They can be used on their own or as supplements to the present volume.

A deficiency with these publications, and it is a natural and expected one, is that they do not make judgements or give specific recommendations. Even when a rating scheme has been initiated, as it has in the area of accommodations, the resulting system does not give a specific recommendation or as much information as you need to make a truly informed decision. (Not all two star establishments are the same from the point of view of personal quality, good food and cheerful hosts. I would, in some instances, rate several establishments which have received one or no stars far higher than several which have received two stars or higher.)

When I first started to travel Newfoundland good places to eat and to stay were few and far between. Most were with poor service and greasy or deep fried food. Anecdotes of these inadequacies abound (e.g., my father-in-law ordered a scotch and soda and after several minutes during which he heard hurried consultation in the kitchen the waitress appeared with a glass of scotch and a box of Cow Brand Soda on the side.) Those places which were good were known to only a few and their reputation was spread by word of mouth among frequent travellers — which I was at the time. Over the years accommodations, service and food have improved considerably and today the hotels and larger motels offer a quality of service which would compare favourably with that found in most parts of North America.

In my recommendations therefore I shall not single out any of these for special praise or condemnation. Instead I shall indicate those smaller establishments which I favour. There is still considerable variety in their quality and some would not be well known outside of their immediate area so I'll mention those which you would not likely find without my advice.

My recommendations give you information concerning where I would travel, where I would eat and where I would stay. These are positive recommendations in the sense that I am recommending the routes which give me the most pleasure, the places where I most enjoy eating and the places where I love to stay. I do not recommend a route or an establishment that I have not visited myself (but on rare occasions I do recommend on the bases of glowing reports from several friends whose judgement I trust). However this does not mean to imply that places which I do not recommend are inferior in any way. It merely means that I have not had the opportunity to visit all of the establishments in Newfoundland and likely have missed some very good ones. You should, of course, feel free to ask for informal advice concerning places which have a good local reputation. You may well find some very fine spots — and more power to you. However, you have my personal guarantee that you will not be disappointed and will find the quality uniformly good for any of my recommendations which you do accept.

What to Expect from your Visit to Newfoundland

Over the past twenty years, as I have travelled in Newfoundland and have become more active as a tour organizer and advisor as well as tour guide, I have met and talked with thousands of visitors to the province. Virtually without exception these visitors report as they leave that they have enjoyed their visit tremendously and spontaneously describe Newfoundland as "Canada's best kept tourism secret." Many return for further and longer visits and encourage friends and relatives to visit as well.

In conversation with these visitors three topics emerge as favourites for comment and speculation:

1. The extraordinary beauty and variety of the scenery — as well as the clarity and wholesomeness of the air and the purity of the water.

2. The surprise in finding that Newfoundland was not at all what they had expected, or had been led to expect, from recent reports on the news media concerning life and times on "The Rock."

3. The warmth, hospitality and friendliness of the Newfoundland people.

I shall comment briefly on each of these topics.

[Incidentally, although today the term "The Rock" is used even by Newfoundlanders to describe our province, that particular use of the term is of recent origin. In my formative years "The Rock" was used much more accurately and appropriately to identify a far more prominent rock: Gibraltar.]

The Beauty and Variety of the Scenery

Few areas of the world can boast such a richness and variety of natural unspoiled beauty as the province of Newfoundland. Majestic mountains and fiords may be found in abundance on the Northern Peninsula of the island, the coast of Labrador, and the south coast region of Bay d'Espoir (pronounced "despair"). Long stretches of glistening white sandy beaches greet the visitor at such places as Cape Race, The Eastport Peninsula and the Northern Bay sands. Breathtaking seascapes with salt water raging up the weathered cliffs on stormy days, or lying placid and brooding on civil days, may be found almost anywhere in the province — but most spectacularly in the marine drive around St. John's and in the areas around Twillingate, Bonavista, and Port de Grave. Frequently the visitor will find a true gem of a view in Bonne Bay, Salvage, Port de Grave, Placentia, Tors Cove and, of course, my favourite Trinity.

As you drive across the island, the variations, sometimes dramatic, in the changing scenery are obvious and impressive. On the west coast the mountains are lofty and majestic: impressive pastoral valleys slope gently between the sheltering peaks; the huge expansive lakes and raging rivers are sufficiently large to float huge drives of logs and to provide a paradise for salmon and trout fishermen. On the east coast the scenes are designed on a smaller scale. The high lands are identified as hills, not mountains, the bodies of water are ponds rather than lakes and the running waters are known as streams or creeks rather than rivers. The central portion of the island is a buffer zone between the two and away from the seacoast the scenery can appear tedious and drab although the wide rivers — the Indian River and the Exploits to name just two — and the majestic stands of birch offer scenes of water-coloured beauty.

The variety of the Newfoundland scenery is not chaotic or haphazard — there is an order and coherence to it. The reason for this has been discovered, researched and written about in relatively recent years by geologists. Many find Newfoundland a rich and fascinating place for their research and some refer to the province as "The Eighth Wonder of the World." The key to the variation in the Newfoundland scenery lies in the theory of Continental Drift, which was first and most eloquently presented by Dr. Tuzo Wilson of the University of Toronto. The theory, in its simplest terms, proposes that hundreds of millions of years ago two continents, the North American and an ancient Afro European continent, came or drifted together, remained together for several millions of years and then moved or shifted apart again. As the continents gradually pressed together, the floor of the ocean which separated them was pushed above the surface of the water. Then as the continents separated again, a portion of land that had originally been part of the Afro European continent was left still attached to the North American continent (a territorial gain).

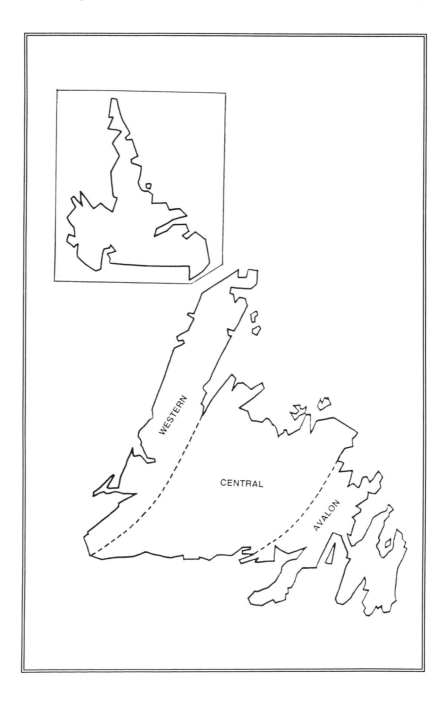

Thus the province of Newfoundland includes three distinct geological regions. The eastern part of the island (incidentally including the Grand Banks) consisting of the Avalon, Burin and Bonavista peninsulas are parts of what was the Afro European Continent. The central part of the island is essentially the sedimentary rock which made up the ocean floor.

The Western part of the province presents a greater complication. (See Map). Most of the western part of the island and Labrador is part of the Appalachian range of North America. However, part of the old ocean floor was thrust upward and westward and now provides some of the spectacular scenery around Corner Brook and Bonne Bay. It provides a shelf of ancient bedrock onto which the more recent mountains were superimposed.

This short summary provides the basic essentials for understanding Newfoundland scenery. However the divisions are not quite as neat and clear cut as has been suggested. There are areas of obvious overlap and irregularity. Also, much later the ice age left Newfoundland scoured with scenic fiords and deposited many moraine deposits and spectacular "perched" rocks.

So remember, when you visit Newfoundland you in fact visit three separate and distinct geological regions. No wonder the scenery is so diverse and compelling.

Why the Surprise?

Visitors almost always report that Newfoundland is not at all like they expected. Undoubtedly influenced by one sided media reports, which highlight natural and economic disasters, they anticipated finding ramshackle unpainted houses, falling down shacks, poorly dressed and badly nourished children, and indolent and depressed adults with a sense of gloom and doom pervading all. Instead, they find, to their great surprise, in addition to the natural beauty, well tended and attractively painted houses and properties, well fed, well clothed and obviously happy children, active, hospitable and energetic adults and little evidence of the malaise that they were expecting.

The most obvious factor in explaining the difference between expectancy and reality is the selective emphasis of the media on the worst possible aspects of economic and social life. These isolated events are then taken to be the usual way of life and negative impressions are created and maintained. Since in recent years we have had more than our fair share of bad luck, including the cod moratorium, and its resulting plant layoffs and spinoff business bankruptcies, our misfortunes have been very much in the public eye. But those of us who are close enough to see the whole picture can put the misfortunes in perspective, while those who see only the negative examples are left with a distorted image. Not only do media reports pinpoint the bad, they almost never include the positive and undramatic aspects. For example, as the noted authority on violent crime, Dr. Elliott Layton, has pointed out, Newfoundland has a crime rate that is far below any other province in Canada and indeed one of the lowest in the world. (The Royal Newfoundland Constabulary, like the British 'bobbies,' are unarmed.)

The roots of this characteristic again go back centuries. Most of the early immigrants were English or Irish, in almost equal numbers, and although certain areas were virtually restricted to one racial origin, in many communities the English and Irish lived side by side. Despite the considerable and violent antagonism which existed in the parent countries, in Newfoundland, the two nationalities, for the most part, rapidly settled down to the business of earning a living, and lived side by side without friction. On a broader level, serious crime was almost unheard of in rural Newfoundland until recently. Few people locked their doors and lost property was returned immediately. Violence, usually in the form of fights at the annual garden party, did occur but was usually blamed on "the liquor" and was not considered criminal.

In recent years there has been an unfortunate increase in thefts, frauds and in various violent crimes but we are still far below the national average. So while you are here relax in the quiet and peaceful atmosphere — but remember to lock your car.

This is not to deny that many Newfoundland families live in what by Canadian standards would be classed as below the poverty line. However, and this is a factor not known "up along," in the Newfoundland outport it is possible to live in reasonable comfort with less actual cash than it would be in the larger centres. Many people own their own homes, provide their own firewood, and grow their own vegetables. Most maintain and repair their properties, and take a sense of pride in the appearance of their buildings.

More to the point perhaps is an observation of John Fraser, who lived in Newfoundland for some years, in a recent article in the *Toronto Sun* —

> I return to (Newfoundland) regularly to keep in touch with the basic values like decency, endurance, loyalty and courage in the face of unyielding destiny. I am always reminded of one basic fact that never seems to be taken into consideration by all the economic aspects, the triumph and stubbornness of a people who have never had a fair chance.

And on a similar view, Ed Smith, one of our favourite present day writers, said in a recent column —

> Despite all the hopelessness permeating the air there are still people whose time and energies are devoted to helping others without thought of recognition or personal gain. Year after year the per capita donation to charitable causes places Newfoundland far above all of the other and more affluent provinces.

There is also the fact that our Newfoundland heritage has conditioned us to accept the bad with the good, to make the best of it with stoicism and without complaint. This theme comes through over and over in our folk songs, like *Tickle Cove Pond*. "The hard and the easy we take as it comes and when ponds freeze over we shorten our runs" (take the good with the bad but take advantage of any favourable circumstance which happens to come along).

Another example of taking what comes with resignation and humour can be found in the lyrics of "Hard Times"

> The best thing to do is to work with a will;
> For when 'tis all finished you're hauled on the hill;
> You're hauled on the hill and put down in the cold,
> And when 'tis all finished you're still in the hole,
> And it's Hard, Hard Times.

The Warmth, Hospitality and Friendliness of the Newfoundland People

Visitors are invariably charmed and captivated by the local people they encounter during their visits. From waitresses to tour operators, to sales clerks to filling station attendants, to youngsters selling berries by the side of the road, visitors note and comment on the agreeable unhurried nature of the Newfoundland way of life and the unique and attractive personality characteristics which it produces. Newfoundlanders who are forced to move away for employment find the people "upalong" cold, impersonal and uncaring. Many hope to move back to the province to recapture the pleasure of working and socializing with fellow Newfoundlanders.

What is it that sets us apart as a people? What elements characterize the Newfoundland personality?

If I had to select three qualities which constitute the essential characteristics of the Newfoundland personality I would offer:
— A sense of friendliness
— A sense of family
— A sense of fun

Friendliness

Newfoundlanders have a well known and richly deserved reputation for friendliness and hospitality. Visitors to the province are invariably impressed by the warmth and consideration of the Newfoundlanders they meet — who will usually go out of their way to provide requested assistance and more. Frequently visitors who ask for directions find themselves drawn into long conversations and are often invited in for a "mug-up" (a cup of tea). Even though many other things about Newfoundland have changed, especially our economic state and prospects in recent years, the habitual warmth of hospitality does not seem to have disappeared or even to have drastically diminished. Almost every week there appears a letter to the paper or a call to an open line show from a visitor who has benefited from the traditional Newfoundland hospitality by way of a friendly welcome, an invitation to meals or accommodation, or loan of utensils, furniture, etc., and all done without expectation of money or reward.

What is the reason for this curious and enduring hospitality? I suppose that one reason may be simple novelty. Visitors to Newfoundland traditionally have been few. Even today, after almost 50 years of Confederation, several decades of television from America, and increased efforts on the part of the Department of Tourism to attract tourists to our shores, visitors are still seen less frequently than in other parts of North America. Also, most visitors are really visiting friends and relatives and do not count as strangers. So novelty is probably part of the explanation. We want to look proper and be on our best behaviour for the benefit of these strangers.

But novelty is not the only factor. There does appear to be a strong and genuine desire to provide assistance for those who are in need. And the assistance is given without reservation or obligation on the part of the receiver to pay or return the favour in any way. These characteristics can be identified from the earliest Newfoundland settlement days and is demonstrated in history and folklore. For example, Art Scammell, the author of the "Squid Jiggin' Ground" reports the following anecdote dating back to the time before the First World War.

> I was fishing at the time with my father and brothers at Change Islands, a Newfoundland outport on the north-east coast. A neighbour ran in to see if we would take a man and his wife, visiting from the city, down to the pier where the steamer on which they were leaving was awaiting them. We agreed at once and father and I jumped in the motorboat and took them to their destination. Just a routine neighbourly act. When we got there the man asked what the charge was and my father said "Nothing." The man pulled out some bills and insisted on paying. "You outport people," he said, "have to learn to move with the times. You'll never get anywhere unless you forget this business of giving your time and effort without getting paid." My father was now getting nettled. This insensitive hangashore not only did not have the grace to accept our hospitality, he was pitting the fledgling philosophy of a pioneer industrial town against the centuries-old tradition of the Newfoundland outport, a tradition of hospitality and kindness to friend and stranger alike. "Put your money in your pocket, young man," said my father. "This place wasn't built on them ideas of yours."

The situation has not changed much since that time and examples of similar experiences may be encountered in virtually every part of Newfoundland, although they are more common in the more remote areas.

The average Newfoundlander will willingly and eagerly go out of his way to provide assistance to any stranger — or indeed anyone in obvious need of help. This aspect of the Newfoundland character is captured in a humorous manner by the following apocryphal story, first told to me by my good friend Esau Thoms.

Imagine that it is the last days of the "Reign of Terror" during the French Revolution. Three convicts, one a Frenchman, one an Englishman and one a Newfoundlander are hustled along to the Guillotine. The Englishman to be executed first is asked, "Do you have any last words?" He replies, "I regret that I have only one life to give for my country." His head is laid on the block. The blade is released and hurtles downward, only to stop one tenth of an inch above his neck. Shaken but alive he is released. Next the Frenchman is asked for his last words and says "My love to my wife and mistress and may they never meet." Again the blade stops one tenth of an inch above his neck and he is released. Finally the Newfoundlander is asked if he has any final words. He surveys the situation judiciously. "Skipper" he says, pointing to the frame of the Guillotine, "I thinks I sees your trouble up there."

There are, however, two minor downsides to this friendly and hospitable behaviour. The first is that the Newfoundlander, in his desire to please, may go overboard in his selection and presentation of information. Thus when a visitor asks "How far is it to such and such a town?" The first thought that may occur to the local is "I wonder how far she would like it to be" — and to give an unrealistically low estimate so that the unsuspecting visitor will find herself driving torturous miles past the expected destination.

The second minor disadvantage is that if assistance is being provided as a favour without any financial recompense then you have to depend on the good will and expertise of the person doing the favour. Since there is no legal obligation on the part of the person doing the service then if it is not completed or is badly done there is no recourse or opportunity for complaint (as there would be if a complete and binding monetary arrangement with its consequent duties had been entered into).

However these are minor cautions and are offered more for theoretical considerations than for practical concerns.

A Sense of Family

It has long been recognized that most Newfoundlanders are reluctant to leave, and that when away virtually all will leap at the chance to return home. This behaviour can be explained in part by the harsh but captivating beauty and serenity of the land, the helpful and cooperative nature of human relationships, and the sense of uninhibited amusement which is ever prevalent. But even more important, I believe, is the disruption in family life which a departure from Newfoundland inevitably brings. Newfoundlanders are exceptionally family oriented. They spend a lot of time in the company of nuclear and extended family members. Even more important, in times of sorrow and trouble they call on and receive help and support from parents, siblings, aunts, uncles and first and second cousins once removed. In olden times, when medical and social assistance were not readily available, the family was the only source of assistance and expertise in the community. The family structure is therefore a stable and enduring source of inspiration and fun during the good times and a source of solace and support during the bad times. Since until recently Newfoundland families tended to be large and concentrated in relatively small geographic areas, family interactions were frequent and easily arranged. Deprived of this family sociability and support, it is no wonder that expatriate Newfoundlanders miss the parties, or the help when a child becomes sick, and that they look forward to a rapid return.

A Sense of Fun

The final characteristic which I believe sets Newfoundlanders apart is a delightful and pervasive sense of fun; Newfoundlanders invariably try to find — and usually succeed — an amusing aspect to every situation in which they find themselves. Since Newfoundlanders do not take themselves seriously (except for some of our politicians) they do not mind — in fact rather enjoy and capitalize on — poking fun at themselves. If, in your travels within, and without (as in St. Jones Without) Newfoundland you find a group who are obviously enjoying themselves in an uproarious and unrestrained manner you can bet your bottom dollar that they are Newfoundlanders. (If not, they are sure to be Australians who share a surprisingly large number of characteristics with us.) I have frequently been a member and participant in such groups of travellers and have enjoyed myself with the rest. On occasion I've been approached by a pathetic and envious feller from the mainland who asked permission to sit in on the group so that he could find out what was so funny.

On a more formal level, Newfoundlanders are born storytellers who delight in weaving amusing stories as well as in telling and retelling old yarns. Superb examples of such storytelling may be found in the writings of Ted Russell, George Earle, Cyril Poole and Otto Tucker. Ray Guy, at his best, is the funniest writer alive today. More recently Buddy Wassisname and the Other Fellers have spread joy and laughter to all parts of Canada. And hundreds and thousands of fans have enjoyed the stage and television skits of Codco, as well as the Gemini award winning "This Hour has 22 Minutes," (See the next chapter: "Wit and Humour" in Newfoundland).

Newfoundland Wit and Humour

Although examples of Newfoundland wit and humour abound in verbal tradition and more recently in a veritable proliferation of written stories and poems, there have been few attempts to classify or to identify the various types of Newfoundland story. A rare exception is *Fun on the Rock*, a theory of Newfoundland humour by Herbert Pottle, but that effort represents more of a scholarly than a practical approach and has not become widely known. Most of our current authors write in their own delicious, unique and distinctive style and the collections of Newfoundland humour are at best a heterogenous grouping of stories that vary remarkably in quality and style.

I attempt in this section to offer a dozen or more examples of the most often encountered types of Newfoundland story. I doubt very much that I will add to scholarship but it may help with the business of finding and identifying the most obvious kinds of stories.

It would be wise at this time to emphasize the vast difference between genuine Newfoundland wit and humour and the oft encountered "Newfie joke." These infamous and nauseating jokes are simply variations on the pathetic, stupid and insulting ethnic jokes which appear variously as Polish jokes, Irish jokes, Italian jokes, etc. At their best they provide some simple and harmless amusement; at their worst they are a malicious and insensitive encouragement to racial and ethnic hatred.

True Newfoundland stories are not only entirely different from their vastly inferior "Newfie" counterparts, they are infinitely more amusing. Newfoundland stories tend to be spontaneous and idiosyncratic. They challenge classification and do not sit well on the printed page. Nevertheless, in an attempt to provide

15

tentative classification, I have culled out a dozen or so from the hundreds that I have read or heard.

Although I can guarantee the complete authenticity of most of these stories in the sense that they were first told by a Newfoundlander in a Newfoundland community, I cannot give that same assurance for all. However each does contain some element which is characteristic of the genuine article.

Several aspects of Newfoundland wit and humour are illustrated.

The most basic are the one liners, the spontaneous quip which seems to summarize and add rich and appropriate associations to a situation in a few well chosen words.

> The Southern Shore is the region of Newfoundland that stretches from St. John's south to Trepassey; the people are primarily Irish and Catholic. From time to time a religious order, in this case the Redemptorist Fathers, would visit the communities in the area to preach a penitential mission. After one such visit an old lady remarked "They were some preachers, them Redemptorists, after they finished their mission there wasn't a mortal sin left on the Shore — or a dollar."

> Two St. John's men were battling their way up Prescott Street one day in June in the teeth of a howling gale and a miserable "dwoi" (or snow storm). One looked plaintively at the other and said "John Cabot got ten pounds for discovering this God forsaken island — he should have gotten TEN YEARS."

> When I attended Memorial University in the early fifties, the Dean of Education was Dr. George Hickman, small of stature but large in confidence and determination. "If a feller gave me trouble in school" he would say "I'd put him out — no matter how big he was — yes he'd go out, even if I had to make two trips with him."

> For years when I was working in the area of Labour Management Relations, I travelled in the company of the late Esau Thoms, a highly regarded labour leader. At that time union officials travelled first class where liquor was plentiful and free. One of the local chairmen was noted for his virtually unquenchable thirst. "Esau," I asked, "how much would so and so drink on a trip from St. John's to Vancouver?" Esau thought for a minute, "Oh," he said, "on a long trip like that one might get as much as 40 miles to the gallon."

Secondly, some stories depend upon the rather peculiar or idiosyncratic use of language in Newfoundland and also our relative unfamiliarity with some of the more modern and technical terms.

Some years ago I was speaking with a colleague at the University who came from the British Isles. He mentioned a certain student and said, "His parents are wealthy aren't they?" "No," I said. For I happened to know that they were as poor as church mice. "That's strange," he said, "the boy told me that his father was taking the car abroad this summer." The word abroad in Great Britain means taking the car to the continent which is usually done by the very wealthy. The word abroad in Newfoundland means taking your car apart piece by piece to repair it and is usually done by the poor.

Not long ago I saw a conflict of cultures — the old and the new — in Deer Lake Airport. An old gentleman, obviously travelling by air for the first time, waited uneasily. When the stewardess asked for passengers who needed assistance to come forward, the gentleman shuffled his way to the front. Not noting any disability the stewardess said "Are you a preboard?" Obviously unfamiliar with the term and the concept, the gentleman said, "Is I a what?" The stewardess could think of nothing better to do than to repeat in a louder voice, "Are you a preboard?" "Oh no missus" he said, "I's a Kelly from Culls Harbour."

We do not take kindly to the metric system with all of its newfangled complexities. Shortly after the system was introduced I came across a small outport store with this sign in the window

Bologna

$1.50 per lb (pound)

$2.50 per km (kilometre)

So if you want to find a store where you can get your winter's supply of bologna at bargain prices I can offer you considerable help.

This may have been the same store which Al Clouston reports on in one of his books. A customer asks for a newspaper. "Ah," says the proprietor "would you be wanting today's paper or yesterday's paper?" "Why today's paper of course." "Well in that case you'll have to come back tomorrow."

Many Newfoundland stories highlight the difficulty which many of us (including politicians) have in understanding the basic principles of mathematics and economics.

In the days when the passenger train (christened "The Bullet" by American servicemen) rounded its way across the island, a foreign gentleman boarded the train in St. John's, and when he disembarked in Port aux Basques he asked the porter "How much should I tip you?" The porter replied "Well now some tips a little and some tips a lot but I spose the average is $5.00." Whereupon the gentleman produced a five dollar bill and handed it to the porter. The porter thanked him enthusiastically and effusively. "Thank you, thank you, thank you, thank you," he said. " 'Tis seldom I gets the average."

A bunch of young fellows in community A discovered that beer was cheaper by 1 cent a bottle in community B, twenty miles away. Every night thereafter they would leave their home community for a night of drinking and carousing in community B. The school master, as school teachers were called in the olden days, decided to give the boys a lesson in the principles of economics. "Boys," he said, "you must take into account the cost of the gas, and the wear and tear on the vehicles and the tires." "Master" interrupted the spokesman for the group, "we knows all that and we makes sure we keeps on drinking 'til we shows a profit."

At the height of Joey Smallwood's power and popularity, Joey determined that he would have a tunnel dug across the Straits of Bell Isle, eleven miles of Atlantic Ocean which separates the island from Labrador. Tenders were called and when examined most required many millions or billions of dollars — all except one. That one was for $224.40. Joey called the bidder into his office and asked for an explanation. "Well," said the bidder, whose name was Bill, "I was told that you should pad a government tender so we did but I'll tell you what we'll do. Two hundred even." "How will you proceed?" asked Joey. "Well" said Bill, "myself and brother George we each got a pick and shovel. I'll start at the Newfoundland side, brother George will start at the Labrador side. When we meets in the middle you've got your tunnel." "Ah" said Joey "but this is a very difficult and delicate engineering feat. How do you know you'll meet in the middle?" "Ah" said Bill after a moment of reflection, "if not then you got two tunnels for the price of one."

On the west coast of the island a visitor stopped to buy a lobster. "How much are your lobsters a pound?" he asked. "Oh" says the fisherman, "we don't sell them by the pound, we sells them by the each" (one at a time). "Well," says the visitor, "How much are they by the each?" "Oh," comes the answer "two fifty a pound."

(Now although that answer may sound nonsensical it is an example of outport wisdom — one cannot select lobsters by the pound, e.g., I'll have two pounds of lobsters — but once selected by the each then they can and should be paid for not by the each because each will vary in size, but by the pound. Very sensible — right?)

And in a similar vein —

A tourist was leaving from Gander airport after a fishing vacation. His luck had not been good and he had caught only one salmon. He was complaining in a loud voice to all within earshot. "Twenty four hundred dollars," he shouted. "Two thousand four hundred dollars for one miserable lousy salmon." "What have you locals got to say about that?" "Skipper" said one of the locals. "You're some lucky you didn't catch a second one."

Finally there are Newfoundland stories which depend on the distinctive use of local terms and expressions. These would mean nothing to visitors unless the terms are explained and will perhaps mean little even after the terms are explained. Each is by a well known Newfoundland author.

From Jessie Mifflin — *Be you a Library Missionary Miss?* (Note: Cross handed means rowing a boat single handed — the oars cross when you lean forward — but by extension it can be used to refer to other activities when done single handed, e.g., I planted my garden cross handed this year.) Ms. Mifflin arrived as a teacher to a small Newfoundland community in the 1930s and proceeded to set up a school choir. One boy had a particularly good voice and she wanted him to sing solo for the Christmas concert. It took her some time to explain what she wanted him to do and when finally he grasped the idea he was instantly appalled. "Oh no miss I couldn't do that" he said, "I couldn't sing cross-handed."

From Herbert Pottle — *Fun on the Rock.* (Note: Early on in the century soft or bituminous coal was available for normal usage and hard or anthracite coal for banking down the fire for the night.) In a small outport the stove in the Anglican church gave up the ghost and as a replacement the congregation bought and installed a used stove from the Methodist (Wesleyan) church. The first morning the stove was used the caretaker could find only the hard coal. The stove did not draw properly and the coals did not light. The caretaker became exasperated. "What can you expect!" he shouted. "In a Church of England church we've got a Wesleyan stove and antichrist coal."

From the master of them all Ted Russell — *Chronicles of Uncle Mose*. (Note: Waterhaul means hauling a cod trap and finding nothing in it but water. So by extension an effort that does not produce any observable result is called a waterhaul.) Pete Briggs had just learned that the new teacher had suggested that John Cabot had landed in Cape Breton rather than in Newfoundland. Pete took it so hard that he decided to investigate. But somehow down deep, I had a suspicion that Pete must have some special reason for gettin' so worked up about John Cabot, and I watched my chance till I got him ... just the two of us. Then I said to him, "Pete", I said, "what odds about John Cabot!"

"Why," said I, "I mean, if they want him up in the mainland, let 'em have him. After all, there's more of them than us, so if they're as anxious to have him as they appear to be, we can't save him."

He looked around to make sure there was no one else within ear-shot. "Uncle Mose," he said, "when I went to school, I didn't learn much. But one thing I did learn was that John Cabot discovered Newfoundland in 1497. Now if I've got to lose **that** 'twill mean I made a complete waterhaul of my education. And that's a hard thing for a man to swallow."

Sometimes misinterpretations may arise or be exaggerated by a combination of several words rather than one specific one. For example —

"Come over for dinner next Thursday evening" is a veritable quagmire of possible misunderstandings.

In Newfoundland, next Thursday means the Thursday of next week and not the Thursday of this week — which is this Thursday or Thursday coming.

Dinner may mean the main meal eaten at the middle of the day (12 noon or 1 p.m.), and evening may mean anytime after noon and not after 6 p.m.

So unless you ask for clarification, you could end up in response to the above invitation arriving at the wrong time (six o'clock instead of one), for the wrong meal (supper instead of dinner), and even the wrong week (this week instead of next week).

Travelling through Newfoundland

In this section you will find material of relevance in the major areas of Newfoundland. They are —
1. St. John's — old and new.
2. The Avalon Peninsula.
3. Placentia and Fortune Bays (the Burin Peninsula).
4. The Bonavista Peninsula.
5. Bonavista and Notre Dame Bays.
6. The Southwest Corner.
7. Corner Brook.
8. The Northern Peninsula and Southern Labrador.
9. Newfoundland by Sea.

In each case you will find a brief overview of the area including a map, a brief description of any places of particular interest, and my personal recommendations concerning routes and establishments.

There is no better way to begin this section than by presenting *The Lure of Newfoundland* written by L.E.F. English and the first of the selections from *Historic Newfoundland*.

The Lure of Newfoundland

Come to Newfoundland! It is the cradle of European civilization in North America. It is the region where the Viking adventurers landed in Anno Domini One Thousand and One and named the newly discovered country Markland, or Land of Forest. It is the New Founde Isle of John Cabot who sailed westward from Bristol in 1497 and made his landfall at Cape Bonavista. It has the proud honour of ranking as the first of Britain's overseas colonies, for

21

John Cabot set up the flag of England here and took possession in the name of his sovereign, King Henry VII. And, on the fifth of August, 1583, Sir Humphrey Gilbert reaffirmed this right of British ownership when he claimed the island in the name of Queen Elizabeth I, and on the King's beach in the harbour of St. John's set up the first colonial government of Britain overseas. Here, too, in more modern times, were wrought some of the greatest accomplishments of science. In the year 1866, the "Great Eastern," wonder ship of her day, landed at Heart's Content the first successful Atlantic cable. At Cabot Tower on Signal Hill, St. John's, Guglielmo Marconi received the first wireless signals across the Atlantic on December 12, 1901. From Lester's Field in St. John's the intrepid airmen Alcock and Brown took off for the first nonstop flight from America to Europe on June 14, 1919. And coming down to a still more recent date, it was in the placid harbour of Argentia that Roosevelt and Churchill drafted the terms of the Atlantic Charter.

Newfoundland is indeed rich in history. Its place names boast a dozen different languages, mute testimony of peoples who came and went and left on bay and island and headland records of their faiths and home memories. Here, war's red tide swept in all its fury when Britain and France fought for dominion in North America through many bitter campaigns of the seventeenth and eighteenth centuries.

Here on the wind swept slopes of Signal Hill was finally decided the last battle of the Seven Years War. Ruins of old forts with their ancient cannon may still be seen. At Placentia the former French capital, are ancient tombstones inscribed in the Basque language, the only relics of their kind in North America. In the west, the tourist may still listen to the Acadian language that Evangeline and Gabriel spoke by the Minas Basin, as told by the poet Longfellow in his pathetic story of their sad romance.

Visit the fishing villages, the so called outports of the Province of Newfoundland. Listen to the quaint language of the folk, and hear the English speech, as it was pronounced in Devon and Dorset in the time of Shakespeare. Or, linger awhile in the settlements where are located the descendants of Irish immigrants, and hear the rolling accent of Cork or the rich burr of a Kerry brogue. Ask for a thrilling ghost story or an intriguing tale of pirate treasure, and you have folk legends galore. Or it may be that you would be invited to harken to fairy magic and watch the little fellows dance on the greensward in truly bewitching moonlight. Join in the merry throngs that laughingly tread the reels and quadrilles to the music of the village fiddler. Hear the folk songs of England and Ireland, songs that today are remembered only in the sequestered hamlets on the Newfoundland seashore. Revel in the supreme thrill of realising that the welcome given the stranger comes from the heart of a delightful people who are remarkable above all else as the most hospitable folk in the whole world.

Take a sea trip down to Labrador, the great northern expanse of Newfoundland. The invigorating ozone from the sea is refreshing to the fevered brow of care and is nature's best recipe for restoring colour to the pallid face of the invalid. Gaze enthralled on the rock ribbed bastions of Belle Isle or the two thousand foot sea wall of Cape Makkovik. Marvel at the seaman's skill that guides the steamer through mazes of islands and channels and weaves a sinuous passage from Rigolet to the placid inland sea of Hamilton Inlet. You are in an Empire of the North, just now about to come into its own.

Newfoundland offers all these, and more! For the historian and the antiquarian there are trails of vanished races and international rivalries; for the artist there are scenic wonders of entrancing beauty; for the lover of outdoor sport there are unrivalled opportunities for trout, salmon and tuna fishing and for wild duck, ptarmigan, caribou and moose hunting. The climate is temperate, cooled in summer by winds that sing up from the sea, and moderated in winter by these same winds that on the coast rarely permit zero weather.

We quote from the pen of Lt. Col. William Wood, a noted Canadian author and historian, the following picturesque tribute to Newfoundland and Labrador:

"Newfoundland is an island of the sea, if ever there was one. Nowhere else does the sea enter so intimately into the life of a people — calling, always calling them — loudly along a thousand miles of surf washed coastline, echoingly up a hundred resounding fiords that search out the very heart of the land, whisperingly through a thousand snug little lisping tickles — but calling, always calling its sons away to the fishing grounds and sometimes to the seafaring ends of the earth. "Labrador is a wild land, ruthless and bare and strong, that seems to have risen overnight from chaos, dripping wet ...It is indeed very much as the Great Ice Era left it thousands and thousands of years ago. But even glacial times are modern compared with its real age. Its formation is older, far older than man; it is older than the original progenitors of all our fellow beings, millions of years ago. It is the very core of the great azoic Laurentians, the only land now left on the face of earth that actually stood by when Life itself was born."

Old St. John's — The Downtown Core

Because of its size, importance and complexity the City of St. John's will be presented in two sections — Old Downtown St. John's and The New Extended City. Old St. John's is described extremely well in *Historic Newfoundland*.

Old St. John's — also from Historic Newfoundland

What hoary traditions entwine about the old town of St. John's caressed by the wild Atlantic surge! Its history, as far as can be ascertained from written records, goes back to the time of John Cabot, who, according to English seamen's tradition, entered the harbour on the evening of St. John's Day in the year of our Lord 1497. From the very first years after Cabot's discovery, ships of Western Europe came to Newfoundland to fish, and St. John's was a rendezvous for them all. Captain John Rut of the British Navy described his visit there in 1527, and on board his ship, the *Mary of Guildford*, he wrote the first letter from North America to Europe and sent it home to King Henry VIII by an English ship that was returning with a load of codfish. It was at the suggestion of the same Captain Rut that the King commanded a West Country merchant named Bute to form a colony in Newfoundland. Bute came out to St. John's in the following year and built the first permanent residence in the island. Thus the founding of the town can be said to date from the year 1528.

Jacques Cartier, the famous French explorer, visited St. John's many times. It was there that he met Sieur Roberval in the early summer of 1542 when the latter tried to compel the Breton captain to return with him up the St. Lawrence River. Cartier eluded his superior by slipping out of the harbour at night and sailing back to

France. Sir Francis Drake made St. John's his headquarters in 1585, when he was sent out on a mission from the British Admiralty; he captured many Spanish and Portuguese ships and brought their crews home as prisoners. This was an attempt to cripple the Armada which three years later launched an invasion of England.

Sir Humphrey Gilbert landed on King's Beach on August 5, 1583, and "in the name of Queen Elizabeth I claimed the island as a British possession." Gilbert was drowned on the return voyage to England, but a full description of the expedition was recorded by Captain Hayes, who commanded the *Golden Hind*. He described St. John's as a populous place much frequented by ships. Hayes wrote of the substantial houses of the merchants doing business at the port, and told of a favourite walk along a path leading to the west end of the harbour to a spot called "The Garden," where grew wild roses, strawberries and other fruits in abundance. The path trod by Gilbert and his officers was the well known Water Street of today, which can rightly claim the distinction of being the oldest street in North America.

Here in the harbour of St. John's the fishing ships of half a dozen nations selected their Admirals to keep law and order in those old days of Rut and Drake and Gilbert. The Admiral held office for a week, when another was selected to keep unruly spirits in check. Thus each weekend saw the Feast of the Newly-chosen, and custom demanded that he should invite all seamen aboard his ship and wine and dine the multitude. We can picture the carousal as brown ale and mead of Merrie England mixed with wines of the sunny South, and toasts to home were offered in rude mugs of baked clay held high in horny and unsteady hands while songs of diverse tongues made the welkin ring in boisterous chorus. Rule by fishing Admiral was sanctioned by English law in 1633, when captain of the first ship to arrive in a harbour was to be admiral of such harbour for that season.

St. John's was several times attacked by enemy forces from both land and sea. A Dutch squadron under the famous De Ruyter took the town in 1665 and plundered it. A second attempt was made in 1673, but this time it was defended by Christopher Martin, an English merchant captain. Martin landed six cannons from his vessel, the *Elias Andrews*, and constructed an earthen breastwork and battery near Chain Rock commanding the Narrow leading into the harbour. With only twenty-three men, the valiant Martin beat off an attack by three Dutch warships. Later in the same year, the gallant company defied the attempts of a pirate squadron to raid the town. After these attacks, forts were erected at both sides of the Narrows. In 1689 a large fort was completed, known as Fort William: it stood where the present Newfoundland Hotel looks over the city. A second fort, known as Fort George, was situated at the east end of the harbour. It was connected by a subterranean passage with Fort William. On the south side of the Narrows, there was a third fortification called the Castle.

The town was captured by French troops from Placentia in 1696, and again in 1708. The French burned the town on both occasions and destroyed the forts, carrying the guns to their stronghold at Placentia. After the second capture of St. John's, better and stronger fortifications were built by the English, and garrisons of British soldiers were maintained in anticipation of a renewal of enemy invasion. The town was captured for the last time in the summer of 1762, but it was quickly retaken by British troops despatched from Halifax under Colonel William Amherst. Fort Townshend was subsequently built on a commanding height above the centre of the town, and several strong forts were placed at the top of Signal Hill and at Fort Amherst on the south side of the Narrows. Garrisons were withdrawn from St. John's in 1871, and the fortifications were dismantled by orders of the British Government.

A visitor to St. John's today sees a thriving city that is rapidly spreading to the north and west.

Among the finest buildings may be included the Anglican Cathedral, which is said to be the best example of Gothic architecture in North America, and the Roman Catholic Basilica which, at the time of its completion a century ago, was the largest church in the northern half of the New World. Government House, with its spacious grounds, and the Colonial Building with its massive columns of grey limestone are well worth a visit from the history lover.

There is also a fine Newfoundland Museum which has many features for the historian and the antiquarian. Among these are paintings and tableaux depicting Leif Ericson landing on Markland, Cabot sighting Bonavista, Sir Humphrey Gilbert setting up the first colonial government of Britain, and the *Great Eastern* landing the first cable at Heart's Content. Besides other more modern aspects of North American history, there are relics of John Guy's colony at Cupids, and of Lord Baltimore's mansion at Ferryland. The Museum also possesses the only relics in existence of the Beothuck Indians, a vanished race of Red Men. There is a booth dedicated to old colonial times, and another dedicated to the Innu culture of Labrador. Dioramas of the seal hunt and of the codfishery present unique and picturesque features of Newfoundland industrial life.

In proximity to St. John's are many lovely fishing villages. A half hour's drive by car takes the tourist to enchanting coastal scenery and through the old fashioned lanes lined with homes of the fisherfolk. And if one is of a mind to view more modern sights, there is the new campus of Memorial University, the Arts and Culture Centre and a variety of new schools, churches and commercial and residential developments.

ﻪ   ﻪ   ﻪ

Begin your tour at the Hotel Newfoundland. The original hotel was built close to the site of Fort William. That hotel was demolished and the new hotel was built close to the original site in 1979.

1. **The Commissariat House** was built in 1818 as the administrative centre for the military officers stationed at Fort William. Over the years it has served as a rectory for the Garrison Church and an infirmary for sick children. It was recently restored to its original condition and it is open to visitors during the summer months when it is hosted by students in period costumes who provide topical entertainment.

2. **St. Thomas' Church** was the original garrison church for Fort William. The first church was built in 1699 and the present building was completed in 1836. The lower story owes its extra width to a narrower structure being blown several inches off its foundation during a severe wind storm in 1846. The wider wings were added to prevent a reoccurrence.

3. **Government House** was completed in 1829 as the official residence of the governor. The original estimate of £8700 had

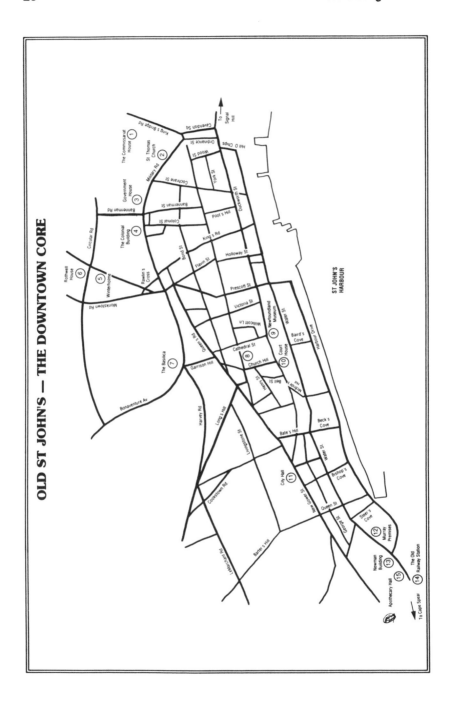

OLD ST JOHN'S — THE DOWNTOWN CORE

to be increased by more than fourfold at the insistence of then Governor Thomas Cochrane. In fact, the house eventually cost more to construct than the White House which was built in Washington during the same time period. Also of note — the house is surrounded by a moat which the architect insisted be included to prevent snakes, reptiles and lizards (none of which are to be found in Newfoundland) from entering the building. Now used as official residence of the Lieutenant Governor, it houses many works of art, including remarkable ceiling decorations by a Polish artist named Pidnikowsky who had been imprisoned for forgery but had his sentence reduced when he agreed to assist with the decoration of Government House and other local buildings.

4. **The Colonial Building** was officially opened in 1850 and was the location for the Dominion and later provincial Governments from 1855 until 1955 when the present Confederation building was opened. Over the years the building was the site of four serious riots and several minor ones, the worst occurring in April 1932 when then Prime Minister Sir Richard Squires was threatened by an angry mob. Today the building houses the Provincial Archives and is particularly valuable for research on genealogy.

5. At the intersection of Bannerman Park/Rennies Mill and Circular Road is **Winterholme**, a magnificent Queen Anne style house completed in 1907 for Sir Marmaduke Winter. It is one of the most expensive houses ever built in St. John's. It was used to house Canadian officers during the Second World War and today continues its life as a Bed and Breakfast.

6. **Rothwell House** opposite Winterholme owes its fascination to two eccentric sisters who together built the house but insisted that no feature should be common to the two halves. The left half is Gothic style while the right is Second Empire.

7. **The Basilica of St. John the Baptist** is the principal Roman Catholic Church in the province. Built on a site selected by Bishop Fleming for its prominence, it was completed in 1855 and was at that time the largest Roman Catholic church in British North America. The style is Roman and the recently

redecorated interior is splendid and colourful. Among the many treasures to be seen are Hogan's "The Dead Christ," and the statue of "Our Lady of Fatima" presented by Portuguese fishermen in 1955. Clustered around the building are schools, convents and monasteries built on the land obtained by Bishop Fleming from Queen Victoria in the 1840s.

8. **The Cathedral of St. John the Baptist** is the principal Anglican Church in the Province. The first wooden structure was built on the site in 1720. The present building, which was completed in 1880, suffered serious damage in the 1892 fire. The building is a superior example of Gothic architecture and was designed by the distinguished British architect Sir Gilbert Scott (who in fact never visited Newfoundland). The building has been almost completely restored but work is still continuing and the spire in the original design has never been completed. The cathedral contains beautiful examples of stained glass and an interesting museum.

9. **The Newfoundland Museum** is located at the bottom of Church Hill on Duckworth Street. It has been a public institution since 1871 and was formerly the Gosling Memorial Library. The present building was erected in 1907 on the site of the Athaneum, the town's first cultural institution. The Museum houses many artifacts from the province's past which can be viewed from 9:00 a.m.–5:00 p.m., six days a week. Generally the museum puts on a temporary theme show for six weeks period at a time. Theme topics have included "Life in St. John's 50 years ago" and "The Lives and times of the Beothuks."

10. **The Court House** was finished in 1901 and has recently been completely restored. The building contains a jail and a variety of courtrooms. Most of the prominent criminal trials are held in one of the court rooms as are ceremonies of admission to the bar and the conferring of the QC. Public executions were held on a scaffold from the Market House on the opposite side of the Court House steps. The last public execution took place in January 1835 when John Flood was hanged for highway robbery.

11. **City Hall.** The seal of the St. John's Municipal Government is located in here on New Gower Street. In 1970 the council moved to this then brand new building and since then a new annex has been added, containing a tourist information office. Historical artifacts and local works of art can also be seen.

12. **The Murray Premises.** This warehouse was restored in 1977 to look much as it did at the turn of the century, when both sides of the harbour were lined with dozens of similar warehouses and the harbour was filled with sailing ships of all sizes and types. The Murray Premises contains boutiques, a specialty liquor store, business offices and a fine art fair each December.

13. **The Newman Building** reflects a colourful segment of Newfoundland's past. The Newman family owned a wine plantation in Portugal which produced a fine port. One year a vessel was lost and the next year found in Newfoundland. Surprisingly the flavour of the wine had improved. Thereafter the Newmans seasoned their port in caves in the southside hills of St. John's before shipping the casks to markets worldwide. The bravery and seamanship of the Newfoundland crews earned the Newman family the right to fly the white ensign — the official flag of the British Royal Navy — over their premises. The Newman family no longer does business in Newfoundland and the building now houses the Newfoundland and Labrador Arts Council.

14. **The old railway station** was opened in 1903 as the eastern terminal of the Newfoundland railway. The design has many Victorian features and is similar to railway stations in many Canadian cities. When passenger service on the railway was terminated by CN in 1969 and replaced by a bus service the building became a bus terminal. The statue in front is called Industry; the model was a Ms. Quinlan from Holyrood.

15. **Apothecary Hall.** In 1982 the Newfoundland Association of Druggists restored an old pharmacy building as a site for a turn of the century Apothecary hall. Open during the summer, in it one can see medicines being prepared and a "drug store" as it actually appeared and functioned in the late 1800s.

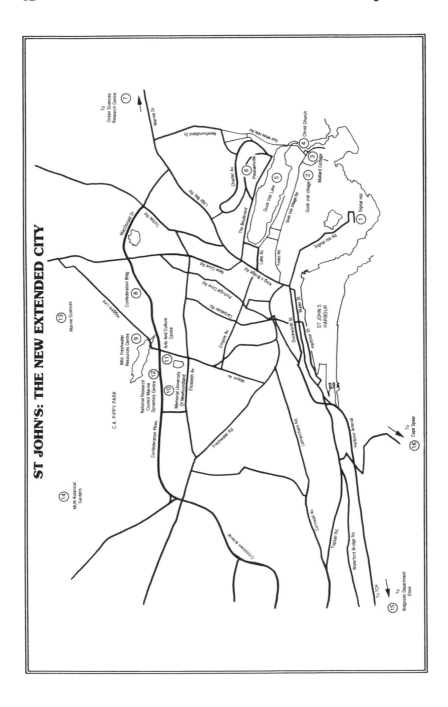

St. John's: The New Extended City

Since 1955 the population of St. John's has more than doubled to over 100,000 and its area has increased ten fold. The old boundaries of the City — Empire Avenue, Road Deluxe and Kennas Hill — are now lost in the maze of newer streets. Towns which bordered on the city are now within its limits and sections which were part of the primeval forest in 1955 are now replete with curbs, gutters and modern bungalows. Memorial University of Newfoundland, which had a student population of 800 before it moved to its new campus in 1961, now boasts a population of 17,000. Other institutions have increased correspondingly. The government, which in 1955 was comfortably housed in the Colonial Building, now fills the entire Confederation Building together with its new annex and more than a dozen buildings all over St. John's. The prosperous business core of 1955 now wears a somewhat shabby and lonely look as old businesses have closed or moved and new businesses are concentrated in the malls which have sprouted up on the outskirts of the city. New schools and hospitals proliferate and a luxurious Arts and Culture Centre provides a venue for musical and theatrical offerings. New modern superhighways funnel ever increasing volumes of traffic into and out of the city while more superhighways are on the drawing boards. Curiously, the city appears to boast more greenery than it did in the early 1950s. The downtown portion of the city, however, still retains the authentic seafaring look that it has had for hundreds of years.

Places of Particular Interest

1. **Signal Hill.** A spectacular promenade gives a magnificent panoramic view of the city and its surroundings. It was from here that in previous centuries messages were exchanged with ships outside the harbour by signal flags. At a location below the brow of the hill, Marconi, in 1901, received the first transatlantic wireless message. Exhibits placed at strategic points on and around the hill identify and illustrate episodes in its colourful past. The last battle of the seven years war was fought here in 1762. Below the hill on most afternoons during the summer season the Military Tattoo provides a realistic

reenactment of battles fought during the many years in which the French and English struggled for possession of North America. Cabot Tower was opened in 1897 to commemorate the 400th Anniversary of Cabot's discovery of Newfoundland. A similar tower was opened in Bristol at the same time on the site of the beginning of Cabot's voyage. The Signal Hill National Park receives more visitors than any other national park in Canada. A well designed walking trail curves around the Hill and into the Battery, and links into a network of trails paced throughout the city.

2. **Quidi Vidi Village.** A typical fishing village on the immediate outskirts of St. John's. Here you will see a fine natural harbour with its entrance further guarded by an artificial breakwater. The fishing premises, consisting of wharves, stages and flakes are similar to these found in hundreds of fishing villages which for centuries dotted the Newfoundland coast. The Quidi Vidi Battery which overlooks the town was erected by the French in 1762 after they had used the town as an entry point for a successful attack on Signal Hill. It was occupied by the British after the peace treaty until 1870 and was completely restored in 1967. Guides dressed in period costumes welcome visitors to the site during the summer months.

    2a. **Mallard Cottage.** Said to be the oldest cottage in North America. The building boasts a fine Mansard roof and very low beams and ceilings. It now houses a fine souvenir shop.

    2b. **Christ Church.** Now converted to a private residence, it was for many years the scene of activities associated with major triumphs and disasters. It was here that scenes for the first North American movie were shot by a film crew headed by Victor Frizzel. Frizzel died the next year when his vessel (*The Viking*), which he was using to gain more authentic seal hunt footage, blew up.

3. **Quidi Vidi Lake.** This large and scenic lake is the site of the annual St. John's Regatta. This race of six oared, fixed-seat shells has been rowed annually (with minor interruptions, due to war) since its inception in 1826. Hence its claim to be the

oldest continuous sporting event in North America. The races are held on the first Wednesday in August or the first fine day thereafter. With sideshows, games of chance, a carnival atmosphere, and attendance rates of 50,000, the Regatta has been accurately described as Newfoundland's biggest and best garden party.

4. **Pleasantville.** A large, cleared area on the side of the lake. During the early months of the First World War the recruits of the Newfoundland Regiment were billeted and trained here before being sent to Europe. In 1919 Alcock and Brown assembled the Vicker's Vimy in which they became the first to fly nonstop from North America to England. (The plane did not actually take off from Pleasantville but from Lester's Field in the west end of the city.) During the second world war, after the U.S. had become a participant, the area (renamed Fort Pepperell) became the headquarters of the North East Air Command. Fort Pepperell continued as an American base until the early 1960s, and during this time at least 10,000 Newfoundland women married U.S. servicemen. Today the buildings have been taken over by the provincial government and house apartments, government offices and Newfoundland's only children's hospital.

5. **The Ocean Sciences Research Centre.** An exotic collection of buildings located in a spectacular setting on the rugged cliffs which jut into the sea. The centre is about ten to fifteen minutes drive from downtown St. John's on Marine Drive off Route 30. The centre was established to provide a research environment in which many forms of marine life including cod, mackerel, squid, seals, scallops and mussels could be studied. The faculty has received international recognition and the centre is considered to be one of the finest in the world. Guided tours are available daily during the summer months. Also during the summer, the MUN Drama Club uses this site to present *Shakespeare by the Sea,* a full length production staged twice a week. Tickets available on site. Warm clothing and extra blankets are suggested.

6. **The Confederation Building.** Opened by Louis St. Laurent in
    1960. At that time the twelve storey building could contain the
    entire provincial government executive and administrative
    staff. Today the government and its employees have flowed
    over into an adjacent annex and many buildings scattered
    throughout the city. Two statues on the grounds are notewor-
    thy. Directly across Prince Philip Drive stands Gaspar de Corte
    Real who visited Newfoundland in 1501, the first European
    explorer after John Cabot to do so. On the lawn to the left front
    of the building is a statue of Dr. Wilfred Grenfell, the well
    known physician who started the Grenfell Association which
    brought health care to northern Newfoundland and Labrador
    in the early 1900s.

7. **The Newfoundland Freshwater Resource Centre.** Better
    known as "The Fluvarium" it is a modern attractive building
    on the north side of Long Pond - just across from the Univer-
    sity. The building was erected at a site where a stream rich with
    marine life enters the lake. The underwater viewing windows
    provide an unusual and exciting view of freshwater marine
    life in its natural habitat. In addition there are displays, exhib-
    its and interpretative programmes which illustrate fish hatch-
    ery, species development and freshwater ecology. The
    Fluvarium is the only facility of its type in North America
    which is open to the general public. Tours are available year
    round.

8. **Memorial University of Newfoundland.** In 1925 the govern-
    ment of Newfoundland created Memorial University College
    which offered the first two years of Arts and Science pro-
    grammes. The College was soon amalgamated with the Nor-
    mal School and offered teacher training programmes. After
    Confederation in 1949 the College was granted degree grant-
    ing status and became Memorial University of Newfound-
    land. In 1961 the University moved from its original location
    on Parade Street to its present location on Elizabeth Avenue. In
    1975 a donation of land permitted considerable expansion and
    the addition of professional schools. Today the university is
    the largest east of Quebec with 17,000 full and part time
    students. The University offers graduate programmes includ-

ing Ph.D. in most academic areas. The institution is world renowned for its studies in marine history and biology, geology and folklore and its pioneering work in distance education and telemedicine.

Adjacent to or affiliated with the university are three other institutions —

9. **The Arts and Culture Centre.** Built by the Provincial Government as a Centennial Project in 1967. The main first class theatre seats 1000 and provides a venue for major local artistic presentations as well as visiting shows. In addition there is a basement theatre, used primarily for experimental theatre, rehearsal rooms, a restaurant, a bar and three libraries. A large portion of the space is occupied by the Newfoundland and Labrador Art Gallery; one of its rooms contains a permenant exhibition of work by the province's most prominent visual artists.

10. **The National Research Council Marine Dynamics Centre wave tank.** Although located on the university grounds, it is owned and managed by the National Research Council. The building is a highly rated facility for studying the behaviour of ships through the water and especially through ice fields. Basic research is supplemented by applied research in which ship and oil companies receive advice for construction and transportation problems. Other "wave tanks" are located in Memorial's Engineering school and the Marine Sciences Institute.

11. **The Fisheries and Marine Institute.** Established in the early 1960s as the Fisheries College. It was at first located in the buildings vacated by the university and later moved to a new location on the hill behind the city. It offers certificate and diploma programmes in many areas of marine and nautical activities. Recently it has become a part of the university and in 1995 the first degree programme was approved by the University senate.

12. **MUN Botanical Gardens.** Located in Pippy Park, a five minute drive from the University, on Mount Scio Road. The

gardens have been developed over the past twenty-five years and now include a wide selection of plants and flowers from all areas of Newfoundland. Exhibitions are presented at regular intervals and guided tours are available during the summer months.

13. **Bidgoods Department Store.** Located on highway 10, just where the road to Petty Harbour turns off. In addition to being a large modern supermarket, Bidgoods offers a "Cove" section, including a wide variety of local products. Here you will find many species of fish, caribou, seal and rabbit meat and many types of jams, jellies and preserves. Few people leave Bidgoods without making a purchase.

14. **Cape Spear.** A national historic site, this is the most easterly point in North America is nearer to Ireland than to Vancouver. Many visitors take advantage of the opportunity to 'turn their back on North America' for a picture. There are gun emplacements from the second world war and the lighthouse and the lightkeeper's house are open to visitors. The lightkeeper was a member of the Cantwell family from 1834 until the lighthouse was no longer in use. The Cape is ideal for whale watching during the summer months. The guides will show you the best viewing sites. During the summer, reknowned local artists such as Anita Best give evening performances in the bunkers. Dress warmly and bring a blanket!

My Recommendations

- Go to the top of Signal Hill by day or night or both. If adventurous walk the North Head Trail.
- Visit the Ocean Sciences Research Centre and continue on the Marine Drive to Flatrock (see the Grotto where Pope John Paul II blessed the fleet in 1984).
- Drive to Bidgoods, a thriving supermarket whose wares include rabbit or seal flipper pie and various other local delicacies. Turn off on Route 10 and proceed on through Petty Harbour to Cape Spear and return via Shea Heights.
- Walk the Rennie River's Trail.
- Visit the Fluvarium or Freshwater Resource Centre where underwater windows offer a view on marine life.

- Arrange a tour of the Marine Dynamics Centre.
- Take a leisurely walk through the Botanical Gardens.
- Tour the Basilica and the Cathedral of St. John the Baptist.
- Spend a leisurely hour in Bowring Park.
- See a play at the LSPU Hall.
- Consider making a pub crawl on George Street or better yet visit the best pubs in town — The Ship Inn, 267 Duckworth Street, and the Duke of Duckworth, 325 Duckworth Street.
- Visit O'Brien's Music Store for the best in Newfoundland Irish music or Freds Music Store for the latest in the Newfoundland traditional, rock or alternative categories.
- In season, see the caplin rolling in the beach in Middle Cove (mid June to early July).
- Take in a performance of the Signal Hill Tattoo (July–August).
- Attend the Folk Festival in Bannerman Park (early August) and the annual Regatta — the first Wednesday in August or the first suitable day (fine with light winds).
- Take in a performance of Shakespeare by the Sea, staged twice weekly during the summer. Tickets available on site on Marine Drive.

Places to eat and overnight —

All the major chain hotels have sites in St. John's and their ratings are given in the Newfoundland Tourist Guide. (Price range $100 to $150, breakfast not included)

But the more budget conscious (or adventurous) might prefer one of the many excellent Bed and Breakfasts. Price range $50 to $85 per person per night, breakfast included (some of the more elegant are more expensive).

To eat (general)—

- The Woodstock Colonial Inn. Most famous for its exquisate local dishes.
- Try the Seafood Galley, singled out by En Route's restaurant guide as one of Canada's top restaurants...
- Bistro 281. A relatively new but highly rated restaurant.
- Looking for Mexican? Try Casa Grande.
- Bianca's on Water Street serves excellent food. Included in Canada's top 100 restaurants.

- The Faculty Club at Memorial. Open on week days during academic terms.
- The Cellar, excellent food and a cozy atmosphere.
- Green Sleeves — part of the George Street Pub scene.
- Ports of Food. Several of the usual fast order counters but the view of the harbour is excellent.
- Stella's has a wonderful atmosphere, and very good food (especially the sea food) at very good prices.
- The Stone House has a solid reputation for serving fine, often innovative, local cuisine.

For ethnic dishes—

- Chinese The Magic Wok
- Indian India Gate
- Mexican Case Grande
- Italian Bruno's, excellent food and first rate service

The Avalon Peninsula

As far as Newfoundland is concerned the cradle of civilization is the Avalon Peninsula. The earliest authorized British settlements were located at Cupids, 1610 (John Guy) and Ferryland, 1621 (George Calvert). The French capital was established in Placentia — which was the centre of French administration for the fishery and the starting point for raids against the English settlements until the treaty of Utrecht gave ownership of the entire island to England in 1713. The peninsula played a very important role in communications with the arrival of the first successful transatlantic cable at Heart's Content in 1866. Air transportation saw Harbour Grace as the site for the setting of many aviation records - including the first solo flight of Amelia Earhart — in the late 1920s and early 1930s. A few years earlier Trepassey was the starting point of the first transatlantic flight when in 1919 an American navy flying boat flew nonstop to the Azores. In 1941, Winston Churchill and Franklin Roosevelt met just north of Placentia on board *The Prince of Wales*, and signed the Atlantic Charter. South of Placentia is the world famous bird sanctuary — Cape St. Mary's. Other and more accessible sanctuaries are located on the bird islands just south of St. John's off Witless Bay and Tors Cove.

Places of Interest

1. **Bay Bulls.** Bay of the Bulls, so called because of the great bull walruses that at one time frequented this harbour. During the French-English wars the harbour was the site of several fierce battles as the French fought their way to St. John's. Today Bay Bulls with its neighbouring community of Witless Bay offers boat tours to the bird islands which are world famous for their populations of puffins, gulls, kittiwakes and other bird species.

2. **The Witless Bay Ecological Reserve (Bird Sanctuary).** Off the coast of the Southern Shore at Tors Cove. This is a must for nature lovers. During the summer several tour companies operate from Bay Bulls and Witless Bay, with each running four of five trips each day. Cost may vary according to the size

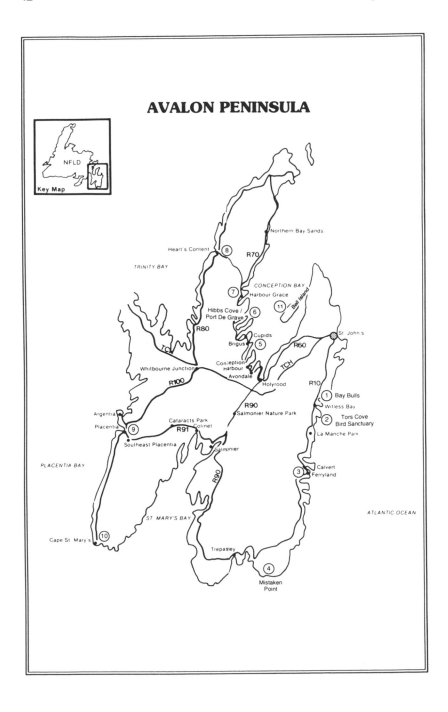

AVALON PENINSULA

NFLD

Key Map

Northern Bay Sands

Heart's Content (8) R70

TRINITY BAY

CONCEPTION BAY

(7) Harbour Grace

Hibbs Cove / (6) (11) Bell Island

Port De Grave

R80

Cupids

Brigus (5)

R60 St. John's

TCH

Conception

Whitbourne Junction Harbour

Avondale TCH

R100 Holyrood

R10

(1) Bay Bulls

R90 Witless Bay

Argentia Salmonier Nature Park (2) Tors Cove

Cataracts Park Bird Sanctuary

Placentia Colinet La Manche Park

(9) R91

Southeast Placentia Salmonier

PLACENTIA BAY

R90 Calvert

(3) Ferryland

ST MARY'S BAY *ATLANTIC OCEAN*

Cape St Mary's (10)

Trepasley

(4)

Mistaken

Point

of groups. Both communities are less than an hour's drive from St. John's along the Southern Shore Highway (Route 10).

3. **Ferryland.** During the past few years the site of the former colony of Lord Baltimore has been under exploration. Established in 1621 and occupied by Baltimore before he went on to colonize Maryland, it is currently the most active archaeological dig in North America. Artifacts are unearthed at a rate of 500 per day during the summer. The location includes an Interpretation Centre, a field house where artifacts are brought for cleaning, sorting and reconstruction and several excavations as well as a garden and some partial reconstructions of buildings as they would have been in 1621. Gerry Squires, the well known Newfoundland visual artist, spent some years living and painting in a lighthouse here.

4. **Mistaken Point.** So called because from a distance and in a light haze its silhouette bears a remarkable resemblance of that of Cape Race. Ship captains, thinking they had passed Cape Race, ordered a sharp turn and sailed straight into the cliffs of Shingle Head. Recently geologists have discovered some of the worlds oldest fossils embedded in its prehistoric rocks.

5. **Hibbs Cove/Port de Grave.** Located just around the cove from Bay Roberts, these two outports offer an intimate and picturesque setting for travellers to explore a traditional Newfoundland fishing village. Hibbs Cove has its own museum, a one-room school house and a house restored to appear as it did at the turn of the century. Entrance to all three is gained by a small donation and all three structures are within 100 feet of each other. Well worth the trip.

6. **Harbour Grace.** This historic community once rivalled St. John's in size and commercial importance. In the early 1600s it was the hideout of the legendary pirate Peter Easton. By the early 1900s Harbour Grace became an important launching off point for aviators making their first attempts to cross the Atlantic by air; Amelia Earhart was among them. You can visit the actual airfield that they used and learn more of Harbour Grace's extraordinarily rich air history at the Museum on Water Street.

7. **Heart's Content.** In 1866, life in this typical Trinity Bay community changed dramatically when it was chosen as the North American station for the transatlantic cable that carried radio messages from Europe to the United States and the British North American colonies. Messages that used to cross the ocean in several weeks were now transmitted in a matter of minutes. The Cable Station has changed over the years but much of it remains as a museum to the cable and its revolutionary technology. The station suspended operations in 1965.

8. **Cape St. Mary's.** Bird sanctuary located about 200 km from St. John's by way of the Salmonier Line, or through Placentia. The site features nesting areas of puffins, gannets, turrs and gulls and a truly spectacular view from the surrounding clifftops.

9. **Brigus and Cupids.** Cupids was the site of Britain's first officially authorized settlement in Newfoundland when John Guy of Bristol brought settlers out from England in 1610. In 1613 the first non aboriginal child, a boy, was born to Mrs. Nicholas Guie. The colony soon spread out to nearby Brigus which became a local centre for business and mercantile activity in the 1800s. It was the birthplace of Captain Robert Bartlett, the famous Arctic navigator and captain. Among his many exploits Captain Bartlett was the skipper of the vessel which took Peary on his successful voyage to the North Pole in 1908.

10. **Placentia.** For many years the French capital of Newfoundland. The Treaty of Utrecht in 1713 and the Treaty of Paris in 1769 confirmed ownership of the entire island by Britain except for St. Pierre and Micquelon and some fishing rights along the French shore in North-western Newfoundland. The establishment of the American naval base in nearby Argentia in the early 1940s greatly changed the economy and way of life. The Castle Hill Museum and Fort provides an excellent history of the town and a truly inspirational view.

11. Bell Island. The oldest mining community in the Province. In the late 1800s a rich grade of iron ore was discovered and in 1895 commercial mining commenced. At the most intensive phase of mining the shafts stretched out for three miles under Conception Bay and the island had a population of over

12,000. During the 1960s the ore petered out, commercial mining ceased and half of the population moved away.

My Recommendations —

- Take a Bird Island tour.
- Continue on to Trepassey (in late summer you have a good chance of seeing a herd of caribou).
- Continue on and drive through Salmonier and Mount Carmel.
- See the waterfall in the Cataracts Park, and the
- Visit Placentia, especially Castle Hill Park and Museum, and the O'Reilly House (with its exhibition on Placentia Bay Resettlement).
- Take a side trip to Cape St. Mary's bird sanctuary.
- Take another side trip to Ship Harbour to see the Atlantic Charter Memorial, where President Franklin Roosevelt and Prime Minister Winston Churchill signed the wartime agreement in 1941. (Caution, it's a pretty rough ride.)
- Continue on to South Dildo and visit the Whaling Museum.
- Visit the Cable Station Museum at Heart's Content (superb).
- Cross the peninsula and visit the airfield and museum at Harbour Grace.
- See the Fisherman's Museum and one room school at Port de Grave.
- St. Vincent's is a good place for viewing whales.
- Brigus is a true gem with its harbour, tunnel and recently restored Hawthorne House — home of Captain Bob Bartlett. Also do not miss the Cupids memorial to John Guy.
- See the railway museum at Avondale.
- Visit the archaeological site at Ferryland. The dig of Sir George Calvert's 1621 colony yeilds more than 50,000 artifacts a year.
- St. Mary's outharbour boasts a beautifully constructed model of a pre-Resettlement village.

Places to eat and overnight —

- Downs Inn in Ferryland — a restored convent.
- Trepassey Motel in Trepassey.
- Northeast Arm Motel in Dunville.
- Galecliffe in Upper Island Cove — a truly unique experience for eating and overnight.

- Beach Cottage Restaurant in Holyrood (superb view).
- Garrison Inn or Old Rothesay House in Harbour Grace.
- Brookdale Manor in Brigus — good meals and comfortable accommodation for large family groups.
- Conception Tourist Home, Conception Harbour.
- the Soiree Restaurant in Kelligrews.
- Rosedale Manor, Placentia.
- Fong's Motel & Restaurant, Carbonear — good food, excellent service.
- The Ark of Avalon in Ferryland.

Placentia and Fortune Bays

Placentia Bay, "that far greater bay" of Ray Guy's writing, divides itself readily into the upper bay and the lower bay. The upper bay — around the bottom of the bay from Argentia to Marystown — was the scene of the most unpopular and devastating of the resettlement programmes of the 1950s and 1960s. Before that, life centred around the isolated harbours and islands and sustained a moderately successful inshore fishing activity. When communities such as Toslo, Paradise, Broule and the major islands of Long Island, Merashean and Red Island became increasingly difficult and expensive for the government to maintain, resettlement grants persuaded inhabitants to move to larger centres with road connections. Virtually all went to places like Placentia and Come by Chance but expected employment opportunities did not materialize and the social and economic life of the bay was wiped out. In recent years people have been moving back to the islands to resume the fishery during the summer months and some have taken up permanent residence.

The lower part of the bay — from Marystown around the boot of the Burin Peninsula — was not affected by resettlement to any significant degree. The large communities of Marystown, St. Lawrence, Burin, Grand Bank and Fortune still maintain relatively large populations. However, the life of the peninsula has centred around the fishery, specifically the Bank fishery with its magnificent tall-masted schooners. Now that the fishery has been placed under a moratorium the future of the Bank fishery and the communities which depended on it is in serious jeopardy. The Fortune Bay communities of English Harbour West, Belloram, English Harbour East and St. Jacques have also had long and intimate connections with the Bank Fishery.

Less than 20 miles off the tip of the peninsula lie the french islands of St. Pierre and Miquelon. St. Pierre, with a population of 6,000, and Miquelon, with a population less than one quarter of that, were awarded to France by the Treaty of Utrecht in 1713. Since that time the islands have been part of France in every respect, with French the only language and French police, civil service and education. The well preserved French culture, lan-

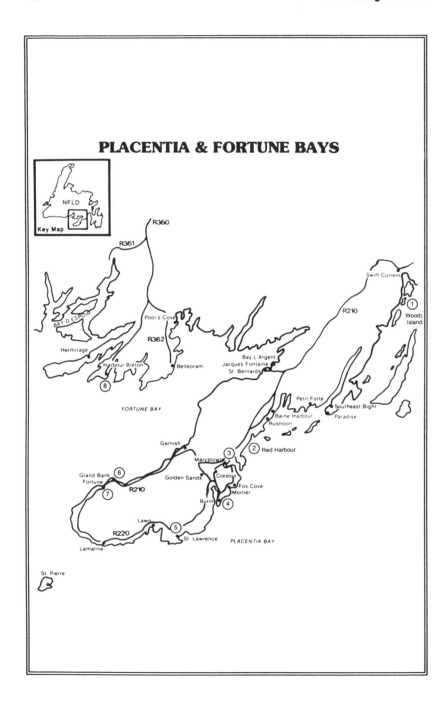

PLACENTIA & FORTUNE BAYS

guage, and customs have made the islands a favourite holiday destination for Newfoundlanders and visitors from away.

Places of Particular Interest

1. **Woody Island**. Like many of the settlements in Placentia Bay this island was deserted or virtually deserted for many years. Recently an entrepreneur who had originally lived in the area built a lodge on the island and offers an "Escape to a Secluded Island" holiday package which has proven to be very popular.

2. **Red Bay**. An example of a resettled community. The people moved on to the mainland from Port Elizabeth on Flat Islands and established a completely new settlement. The first major decision turned out to be the location of a graveyard when an accident on the day of resettlement claimed the life of a teenager. Even today the community does not have the settled permanent appearance of most older Newfoundland settlements.

3. **Marystown**. An old established community with an Irish connection and tradition. Marystown or "Mortier Bay" was promoted for many years as a duty free port in which large transatlantic vessels could transfer their cargo to smaller vessels for delivery up the St. Lawrence River and along the North American seacoast. Nothing came of the idea but in recent years Marystown was selected as the site for a major shipyard and the life of the community has been dramatically changed by that development. More recently the shipyard has become the location for some modules of the construction of the Hibernia platform. At the present time the site teems with skilled tradesmen but the life span of the project is uncertain.

4. **Burin**. One of the oldest settlements on the peninsula and a major centre for business and economic activity. Like many older Newfoundland communities its role has changed dramatically over the years and it no longer occupies the prominent position it once did. The town continues to be one of the best kept and maintained and the area surrounding Burin Bay Arm is certainly one of the most scenic in the province.

5. **St. Lawrence.** A typical Burin fishing community until some 60 years ago. Fluorspar was discovered and commercial mining commenced; the town prospered for some time. During the second world war two American destroyers, the Truxton and the Pollux drove aground on the cliffs close to the town. The heroism of the inhabitants during rescue activities earned the town a gift from the American government — a hospital. After the war, miners began to sicken and die, earning St. Lawrence the designation of the town of widows. Tests confirmed that the mines contained dangerous levels of asbestos and the mines were closed.

   For over a century soccer teams from the Burin peninsula have dominated senior soccer leagues in Newfoundland and in recent years teams from the peninsula have won the Canadian Senior Football Championship.

6. **Grand Bank.** The largest and most typical fishing community on the Burin Peninsula. The town was thriving and prosperous until recent decades. Many of the houses are large, well built, of Queen Anne style, and modelled after houses in Halifax rather than St. John's, which reflected the communication pattern until road communication down the peninsula was established. Some houses include the widow's walk — a second floor balcony where the wives of sea captains could look out on the sea to search for the first sight of their husband's vessels.

7. **Fortune.** Another sea-based community and the Newfoundland terminus of the St. Pierre Ferry. The high speed vessels which operate out of this port can reach St. Pierre in less than an hour. Canadian immigration and customs greet the returning visitor after one or more days on the French island.

8. **Harbour Breton.** Located on what is now known as the Connaigre Peninsula (after Connaigre Bay) this was until the early 1900s the economic and commercial capital of the southcoast from Fortune Bay to Burgeo. A number of English commercial ventures, the most prominent and influential of which was the Newman Company, operated and controlled the area for a century and a half.

My Recommendations.

After you turn off the TCH on to Route 210 through Swift Current —

- Take a side trip to the serene and picturesque communities of St. Bernards, Bay L'Argent, and Jacques Fontaine.
- Take time to tour the Marystown/Creston area and to explore Burin and Burin Bay Arm.
- Go all the way around the boot and visit St. Lawrence, Lawn and Lamaline before continuing on to Grand Bank.
- Take your time to see the old fishing captains' houses and business premises.
- Visit the Fisherman's Museum in Grand Bank.
- The Golden Sands Resort is well worth a visit.

If you wish to visit the communities in Fortune Bay you will have to rejoin the TCH, proceed west and turn off on Route 360 at Bishop Falls. For those with the time and inclination a visit to St. Albans, Hermitage and Belloram can be a rewarding experience (see the chapter Newfoundland by Sea).

Places to eat and overnight —

- Swift Current — Kilmory Resort.
- Grand Bank — Thorndyke Heritage Home.
- Woody Island — Escape to a Secluded Island, or Island Rendevous - an overnight stay in a resettled community. The boat leaves from Garden Cove.
- Head of Bay d'Espoir - Motel Bay d'Espoir.
- Burin — Burin Country Frills Bed and Breakfast.

The Bonavista-Trinity Peninsula

If the Avalon Peninsula was the site of the first official attempts to colonize Newfoundland, then the Bonavista-Trinity Peninsula was the location for the earliest permanent settlements based entirely on the fishery. The peninsula is rich with historical firsts. Cabot sighted land at Cape Bonavista in 1497. Permanent settlements in Trinity date back to the 1500s, probably 1558. Sir Richard Whitborne held the first court of justice in the New World in 1615 and in 1798 the Rev. John Clinch introduced the use of smallpox vaccine in North America. The first school in Newfoundland was established by the Society for the Propagation of the Gospel in Bonavista by a Rev. Jones in 1726. Over the centuries the history of the peninsula has been intimately associated with the coastal and Labrador fisheries. For over three hundred years the major merchant families of South-western England, the Lesters, Slades and the Bremners maintained essential fishing and trading establishments in the area (primarily in Trinity). As late as 1950 a successor to the fishing firm of The Ryan Brothers maintained fishing premises in Trinity and for twenty years after that in Bonavista. Early in this century the domination of the fishing companies was successfully challenged by activist William Coaker who established the Fisherman's Protective Union, with business premises in Port Union. And if history is not sufficient to attract you to the area, the scenery will rival that of any part of Newfoundland. Indeed Trinity is generally considered to be one of the prettiest and best preserved towns on the island.

Places of Particular Interest

1. **Bull Arm.** The site where the huge drilling platform for the Hibernia Oil Field was built. Hibernia was the largest construction site in the world and at its peak employed over 3,000 workers.

2. **Clarenville.** The town was named after the son of Governor Boyle. The town came into prominence in the early 1900s when it was selected as the junction point for the Bonavista Branch

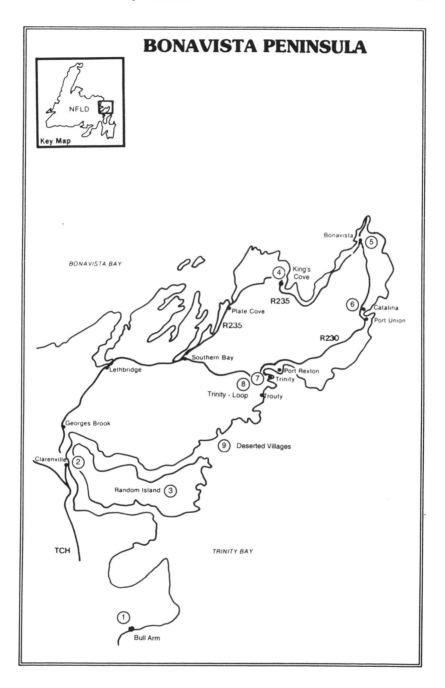

BONAVISTA PENINSULA

Key Map
NFLD

BONAVISTA BAY

Bonavista ⑤

King's Cove ④

R235

Plate Cove

R235

Catalina ⑥
Port Union

R230

Southern Bay

Lethbridge

Port Rexton
Trinity ⑦
⑧
Trinity - Loop   Trouty

Georges Brook

Deserted Villages ⑨

Clarenville ②

Random Island ③

TCH   TRINITY BAY

① Bull Arm

Railway, and today, in the absence of the railway, it continues to be a commercial and administrative centre for the area. In 1929 the Italian aviator Balboa landed a flight of 11 seaplanes in the waters of Random Sound. For the past thirty years the protected waters of the sound have been designated a sanctuary for Canada geese.

3. **Random Island.** The largest island in Newfoundland waters, it provides a home for seven communities. It is joined to the mainland by the Hefferton causeway at Milton. This is where William Eps Cormack began his famous walk across Newfoundland in 1822.

4. **King's Cove.** Known as the "Athens of the North," because a high level of music and scholarship was maintained in the late 1800s and early 1900s. This was primarily due to the foresight of parish priests who identified promising young men and women and sent them away for university studies. They were urged to return to their home town as teachers and several of them did. Because of this, King's Cove is known as the birthplace of many scholarly individuals and business families, including Gerald S. Doyle, J.M. Devine and the Lawtons. Close by is Keels where Cabot is reported to have actually landed.

5. **Bonavista.** Cabot's first sight ("O Buenovista") of Newfoundland in 1497. One of the oldest and largest fishing towns in the province. It is the location of the first official school in Newfoundland. Here you will find the Mockbeggar property, home of the late Senator Gordon Bradley. There's also a most attractive and fully functional lighthouse — the most interesting in the province. Just outside the town you will find "the Dungeon," a cave in which the roof has foundered, or fallen in, so that you can see the sea surging in through the two entrances.

6. **Catalina-Port Union.** Catalina or St. Catherines Harbour was first visited by Jacques Cartier in 1534. Until the 1992 Moratorium it was home to the largest fish plant for processing northern cod. Port Union is a town which was founded by Coaker as the site for his Fisheries Union premises. It is one of

the very few towns outside of the Avalon Peninsula where you will find row housing. You will also find the monument to Coaker — a bust which looks away from the sea.

7. **Trinity.** Invariably described in tourist literature as "A gem ... a national treasure ... a must see in anyone's calendar." Most of the old town is a national heritage community and there are several national historic sites. The buildings are historically intriguing and well preserved. The Roman Catholic church built in 1832 and still in use is the oldest wooden church in Newfoundland. The setting is unmatched anywhere in eastern Canada. In recent years the outdoor play, the Trinity Pageant, a superb addition to any visit, moves through several locations and depicts various scenes from Trinity's colourful past.

8. **Trinity Loop.** When the Bonavista branch was being built the terrain required a rapid change in elevation of the railway tracks. The engineers routed the track for one mile around a pond and then back to cross 60 feet under the arch which contained the higher rail line. The construction was the largest and highest visible loop in North America. Some years ago when the rail tracks were being removed from all over Newfoundland a persistent local effort persuaded CN to leave the rails around the loop. Today the area houses an amusement park which includes train rides.

9. **Deserted Villages.** Almost a dozen villages (Kerleys Harbour, British Harbour, Little Harbour, Pope's Harbour, Ireland's Eye, Traytown, ivanhoe, Thoroughfare, Deer Harbour) which thrived and included a total population of more than 3,000 up until forty years ago are now abandoned. Some of the properties are still in good condition. A walking trail from New Bonaventure can take you to the closest communities and a short boat ride can take you to the remainder.

My Recommendations

Spend one or two days in this area. Leave the highway at Clarenville via Route 230. Turn left at Southern Bay on to Route 235 and proceed to Bonavista via King's Cove in Bonavista. See —

- The Mockbeggar property.
- The recently opened Ryan Premises.
- The lighthouse (excellent).
- The Dungeon (also excellent).

Then on to Catalina and Port Union. Visit the Fisherman's Protective Union property, Coakers Monument and graveyard, and the Railway Museum.

On to Trinity. See —

- the Pageant, and check what productions are slated for the Summer in the Bight theatre festival
- the Anglican and Roman Catholic churches.
- Interpretation Centre.
- The Trinity Loop (marvellous).
- drive out to Fort Point. If venturesome, climb Gun Hill for the most superb view in eastern Newfoundland.

Places to eat and overnight —

- In Clarenville try Marian's European Deli. Excellent German food.
- The Trinity Cabins are the oldest tourist establishment in Newfoundland (1948) and still remarkably popular.
- The Erikson Premises, Trinity offers good food and elegant bedrooms.
- The Riverside Lodge, Trouty (my personal favourite) a warm welcome and excellent food (ask for the pan fried cod).
- The Campbell House in Trinity is Newfoundland's most popular Bed and Breakfast.
- Art Andrews Peace Cove Inn is highly regarded and his Trinity premises includes a restaurant, marina and craft shop (with original art works).
- Greenings restaurant in Lethbridge serves excellent food (try the soup) and the fastest service in North America.
- In Bonavista the several Bed and Breakfasts (Abbotts, Butlers and Whites) are good but a special commendation goes to the Silver Linings.

The Northeast Coast and Central Newfoundland

In many parts of Newfoundland the national origins are mixed, or if one predominates (like the Irish on the Avalon peninsula) there is still a good healthy balance of settlers. On the Northeast coast from Cape Bonavista to Long Point, Twillingate, there is no doubt that the settlement roots are British and Protestant. The Anglican and United Church clergy serve almost ninety percent of the population. The protestant ethic of "a good days work for a fair days pay," with the extra pride in workmanship, ensures even unseen parts of a chair or chest are given as much care as the more visible parts. This was, and to some extent still is, evident in every house, every stage and every wharf. The land is not fertile and many would say that the landscape is bleak and forbidding and yet for more than a hundred years this part of Newfoundland gave evidence in its large stately homes of being the most successful and prosperous in the province. The best known and most successful of our fishing and sealing captains were born and raised and received their early apprenticeship in this area. Massive schooners which were built and crewed by local seamen went to the Labrador and brought back loads of salt bulk cod, or to the ice to return with a bumper crop of seal pelts.

The area also includes central Newfoundland which contains three of the few inland towns on the island: Buchans, one of our best known mining towns; Gander, known in avation circles as the Crossroads of the World; and Grand Falls, Newfoundland's first paper mill town. Grand Falls is virtually in the centre of Newfoundland being 456 km (285 mi) from St. John's and 480 km (300 mi) from Port aux Basques.

Places of Particular Interest

1. **The Eastport Peninsula.** One of the most attractive areas of the province and the location of the first artistic festival in the Province. Eastport was the location of Gerald S. Doyle's (of the Doyle Bulletin and the Doyle Song Book fame), summer home (White Sails). The sandy beach around Eastport is a favourite for summer visitors. Across the peninsula, the town of Happy Adventure boasts some of the largest and sturdiest homes in

NOTRE DAME & BONAVISTA BAYS

Key Map

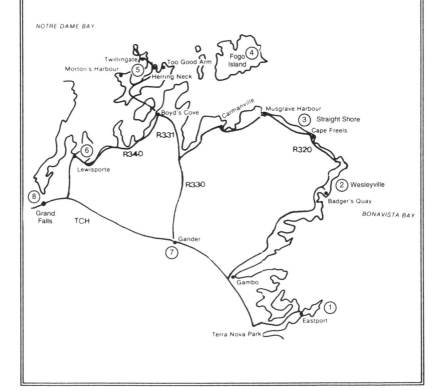

the province. At the end of the peninsula, Salvage, a typical fishing outport, claims a history that goes back to the time of earliest settlement. Near the community of Burnside relics and artifacts from early Aboriginal peoples have been found and are being actively researched during the summer months.

2. **The Wesleyville area.** From this area came the most famous fishing and sealing skippers, the Keans, the Windsors and the Barbours, as well as the highly esteemed artist, David Blackwood. Greenspond, once an offshore island but now connected by a causeway, was a centre of culture and commerce known as "The Hub of the North." Newtown (one of the original centres for resettlement from the islands in the 1800s) offers the magnificent newly restored Barbour house and the Newtown church with its dramatic setting.

3. **"The Straight Shore."** This area between the Bonavista and Notre Dame Bays does not belong to either bay and because of its almost straight shoreline is called the straight shore. It includes starkly dramatic scenery, impressive sandy beaches (Windmill Bight) and one town, Musgrave Harbour. It was close to this town that, during the Second World War, Sir Frederick Banting, the co-discoverer of insulin died in a plane crash (which to this day some think was caused by sabotage).

4. **Fogo Island.** The second largest of the offshore islands, Fogo provides a home to seven different communities. The largest are Fogo, Joe Batt's Arm, Tilting and Seldom Come By. (Curiously Seldom Come By originally referred to the fact that vessels seldom passed by — they almost always stopped — a completely different connotation than the isolation which the name suggests now). The island of Fogo offers a surprising variety of plants and animals and has been used in recent years as the site for nature and ecological studies. A hundred years ago Fogo was the centre of commerce for Notre Dame Bay as businesses already established in Trinity opened branch premises in Fogo. Fogo is served by a ferry which leaves Farewell and calls at Change Islands. Another community famed in song and story, Change Islands, was the birthplace of a large number of well educated and successful individuals.

Art Scammell, one of the most famous, wrote the "Squid Jigging Ground" when he was fifteen years of age.

5. **Fogo-Twillingate-Morton's Harbour** — This circuit was immortalized in the traditional song All Around the Circle. Follow the road to the Isles from Notre Dame Junction and it will take you through New World Island and the communities of Morton's Harbour and Herring Neck — once thriving and prosperous fishing communities. Herring Neck was the site of the inaugural meeting of the Fishermen's Protective Union in which thirty-two fishermen gave Sir William Coaker his first boost of economic and political power. Twillingate is the largest community and the centre for business and governmental affairs. Its fine hospital dates back to the time of Dr. Wilfred Grenfell's colleagues. The best known of Twillingate's children was Georgina Stirling, an opera singer, who earned fame in Milan and other European cities before developing a throat ailment which ended her career while she was still in her mid-thirties.

6. **Lewisporte.** Many individuals have had towns named after them but one man has two communities named after him; Lewis Miller, an entrepreneur after whom both Millertown and Lewisporte are named. Lewisporte was the terminus for the Labrador coastal service but as the service was reduced the marine activity was drastically cut back. There is an active dockyard with ship building facilities and a new and rapidly expanding industrial park. Much of the fuel used at the Gander airport is imported through Lewisporte. The community still remains one of the most attractive on the island.

7. **Gander** is the principal airport town of the province. From modest beginnings in 1938 the airfield attained prominence during the second world war when it was the starting point for the air-ferry command which piloted planes from North America to England. After the war the geographic position - midway between Europe and the major North American cities earned Gander the title of "Crossroads of the World". Today the big jets overfly Gander but the airport is still moderately

successful and the town has become a well-established convention centre.

8. **Grand Falls**. The earliest and most successful pulp and paper operation in Newfoundland. In the early 1900s, the British publishing magnates, Lord Northcliffe and Lord Rothermere predicted a shortage of newsprint and after a visit to the island they decided that the Grand Falls on the Exploits River would provide the necessary power. Accordingly, they formed the Anglo-Newfoundland Development Company (AND Co.) and in 1909 the mill was ready for production. The town of Grand Falls was established to provide houses for the mill employees. Those who were seeking work set up the neighbouring town of Windsor. In 1992 Chatelaine Magazine identified Grand Falls as one of the ten most pleasant towns in Canada in which to live. Recently, the towns of Grand Falls and Windsor voted to amalgamate and today are known as Grand Falls-Windsor. The name of the mill has changed as well and is now known as the Abitibi Price Mill. Today the combined town can boast of the Exploits Valley Salmon Festival, listed as one of the top ten events in North America, and the Salmonoid Interpretation Centre. Also the history of the Beothuk people, who frequented the Exploits Valley is recreated in the Mary March Museum.

My Recommendations
- Visit the Eastport Peninsula and relax on the beaches.
- Explore Salvage and visit its Fisherman's Museum.
- Grab a shovel and help with the dig at Burnside.
- Drive around the loop "from Gambo to Carmanville and on to Gander." This will take you through such celebrated communities as Badger's Quay, Wesleyville (where visual artist David Blackwood was born), Valleyfield and Newtown.
- Take "The Road to the Isles" and watch the icebergs sail majestically past Long Point in Twillingate.
- Take the ferry to Change Islands and on to Fogo. Drive around Fogo Island and note the differences in the various communities. (Tilting is very similar to an Irish village despite the wooden houses.)

- Marvel at Burnstone Head, said by the Flat Earth Society to be one of the four corners of the world.
- In Gander visit the Airport and Aircraft Museum and see the displays of the early days of aviation in Newfoundland.
- See the authentic Hudson Bomber, one of those ferried across the Atlantic during the second world war, which is mounted on a pedestal on Skipper Drive, a short distance from the airport. You might also visit the Silent Witness, a memorial to the 256 American servicemen who died, in 1985, when their plane crashed soon after take-off.

In Grand Falls and Port Blandford visit the —
- Atlantic Salmonoid Interpretation Center — a glass wall permits you to see the salmon as they make their way up the falls.
- Attend the Atlantic Salmon Festival (mid July). One of the most highly rated festivals in North America.
- Visit the Mary March Museum.
- The Twillingate Museum, which has a much material realted to Georgina Sterling, the locally-born singer who became known in Europe and North America as "the Nightengale of the North".
- The Barbour House in Newtown, a newly restored, century old fish merchant's home.

Places to eat and overnight —
- Anchor Inn, Twillingate, a favourite for large tour groups.
- White Sails Inn, Eastport; this includes both cabins and a main house, previously the residence of one of Newfoundland's best know businessmen, Gerald S. Doyle.
- Port Blandford, Terra Nova Hospitality Home offers comfortable accommodations and excellent food.
- Botwood, the Dockside Restaurant serves superb food and for overnight the Blue Jay Bed and Breakfast in nearby Northern Arm.
- and there are major hotels in nearby Gander and Grand Falls.

The Southwest Corner

The southwest corner from Harbour le Cou to the Port au Port Peninsula contains almost as much variety as the entire island. The colourful fishing communities from Rose Blanch to Margaree blend into the sandy beaches around Cape Ray, the high tableland behind Port aux Basques, the unforgettable beauty of the Codroy Valley and finally into the sweeping rural vista of Stephenville and the Port au Port Peninsula.

The town of Port aux Basques has long been considered the gateway to the province. The town had been the western terminus of the Newfoundland trans island railway (later the CN) and the eastern terminus of the Gulf ferry from North Sydney on Cape Breton Island. Port aux Basques has seen many changes in cargo handling from car to car transfer to truck to truck transfer to trailer trucks with no transfer at all. Ferry service has expanded from the original, the *Bruce*, to the ill-fated *Caribou* (sunk by a German submarine in 1942 with great loss of life), to the imposing bulk of the Joseph and Clara Smallwood with its capacity for more than 500 cars and more than 1000 passengers. (Incidentally, Port aux Basques played a little known but important role in the communications area when Samuel Morse — of morse code fame — visited the town and supervised the laying of the first cable across the Gulf in 1856).

The area is home to two unique ethnic groups in Newfoundland, the Scots and the French. Although you will find individuals of scottish descent in every part of Newfoundland, the only collection of genuine scottish settlements in the province is in the Codroy Valley: St. Andrews, Highlands, and McIvers. These Scots came for the most part from Nova Scotia rather than directly from Europe, as did the French who settled many of the settlements on the Port au Port area — De Grau, Cape St. George, Lourdes and Siding Brook. The French came to this area over a hundred years ago and at first remained relatively isolated and undisturbed within their own language and culture. Gradually they began to mingle with the English, to work side by side and to mix socially. The process was greatly accelerated by the coming of the American base and the industrialization of the Stephenville area. Gradually French names were changed to English, the French language was used with less and less frequency, and customs and traditions were forgotten. Some forty years ago, partly inspired by some of the older people in the villages and partly by language and folklore academics from the University, a revival of the French language and culture commenced. French immersion programmes were brought into the schools. French folk festivals and academic conferences were held. Today the area has regained much of the original culture and customs and the French language is used naturally and fluently.

Places of Particular Interest

1. **Stephenville.** An old fishing village which became the site of the large North East Air Command American air base during the early 1940s. The base provided employment and other economic benefits (as well as considerable culture shock) over the next 40 years. Some twenty years ago the base was reduced in numbers and importance and recently closed. During its last days, the Smallwood regime, in an effort to shore up the economy threatened by the phasedown of the American base, set up a "Labrador Linerboard Mill." The mill did not live up to its grandiose expectations and was eventually taken over by the Abitibi Price Company which operated it on a smaller scale in conjunction with its other Newfoundland operations. Recently Stephenville has become well known for its imaginative Stephenville Festival which attracts talented theatre artists for gala performances during the summer months.

2. **Cape St. George.** The centre of the area in which the French way of life is demonstrated in the houses and gardens as well as in the language and customs. During the festival season a visit would be particularly enjoyable and educational.

3. **The Codroy Valley.** Communities of Upper Ferry, Doyles and O'Regans provide unsurpassed views of the Codroy Valley and river against a background of the Long Range Mountains — some of the best scenery in the province. The Codroy Valley also boasts some of Newfoundland's most fertile agricultural land.

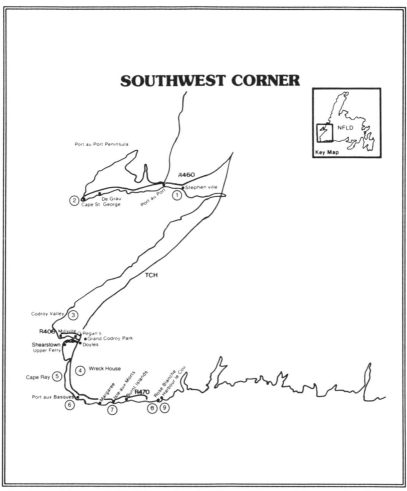

SOUTHWEST CORNER

4. **Wreckhouse**. At this point the Long Range Mountains form a funnel which accelerates the force of the wind and directs it toward the railway bed and the highway which are adjacent to the ocean. In the early days of the century train cars on occasion would be blown off the tracks, over the cliffs and sometimes into the ocean. The man who lived in "Wreckhouse," Laughie MacDougal, developed a keen sense for measuring the force of the wind. The railway retained his services for fifty years and when Laughie phoned the dispatcher to recommend that the train be stopped the dispatcher, without further ado, would order that the train be halted and chained down to

the tracks. After Laughie died in 1965 his wife Amanda continued to act as the human wind gauge until she also died in 1972.
Today sensitive electronic equipment built into the hills and
costing millions of dollars continue (with slightly reduced
efficiency) to do the job for which the MacDougals were paid
$25.00 per year.

5. **Cape Ray Cove.** Known for its beautiful sandy beaches which
    continue for mile after mile. A sight unsurpassed in New-
    foundland, ideal for relaxing and picnicking.

6. **Port aux Basques.** The road and ferry terminus has been
    amalgamated with the neighbouring fishing town of Channel
    to form Channel-Port aux Basques, one of the largest towns on
    the island. Although hundreds of thousands of visitors pass
    through the town each year they rarely see anything except the
    ferry terminal. And yet — on a fine day — a drive around the
    town and the surrounding villages would provide a rich and
    rewarding experience.

7. Along the south coast from Port aux Basques you will find
    several colourful and attractive fishing villages. The most
    noteworthy are —

    7a. **Harbour Le Cou.** The setting for one of our favourite folk
        songs — which you should make sure you hear during
        your stay.

    7b. **Rose Blanche.** Named for the colourful red and white
        cliffs which surround the town and for the colourful array
        of houses which cling to the cliffs and make up the town.
        The prominent lighthouse is one of the oldest on the
        island.

    7c. **Isle aux Morts.** Isle of the Dead — named for the large
        number of wrecks and drownings which have occurred
        over the years. Stories of life saving also abound. George
        Harvey, his daughter Ann, and his Newfoundland dog
        "Harry Man" saved 163 people from one wreck alone. In
        1981 an early navigation instrument — an astrolabe —
        dated 1628, a rare and valuable find, was located by a local
        diver.

My Recommendations

- Drive out to Stephenville and around the Port au Port Peninsula.
- Enjoy the Long Range Mountains and the Codroy Valley from Route 406.
- Remember Laughie MacDougal as you drive past Wreckhouse.
- Just outside Port aux Basques make sure you get an uninterrupted view of the twin mountains.
- In Port aux Basques visit the Interpretation Centre, the Museum, and the Memorial to the *Caribou*, close to the passenger terminal.
- Relax on the Cape Ray Beach.
- Drive through the south coast towns and take a leisurely walk around Rose Blanche.
- Have a leisurely picnic at Barachois Brook Provincial Park.

Places to eat and overnight —

- Dhoon Lodge at Black Duck.
- Hotel Stephenville or Holiday Inn in Stephenville.
- Hotel Port aux Basques (try its excellent fish cakes).
- Christopher Hotel, also in Port aux Basques.

Corner Brook, The Bay of Islands and Bonne Bay

In all of Canada no city has a more beautiful natural setting than Corner Brook. Nature has been lavish in the arrangement of hills, valleys, lakes and bays. Corner Brook itself owes its name to a small brook flowing into the Bay of Islands a short distance from the mighty Humber River. The area consisted of several small fishing villages until the early 1920s when then Prime Minister Sir Richard Squires, in an attempt to "put the hum on the Humber," arranged for the construction of the island's second major pulp and paper mill at Corner Brook. (The first had been established some years before at Grand Falls.) The wood was cut in the interior, floated down the Humber, processed into paper at the Corner Brook mill and shipped overseas. The coming of the railway in the late 1900s had given the town a certain prominence and the additional impetus provided by the mill insured rapid growth. Eventually the town incorporated the adjacent communities and became the second city of the province. (The third city is Mount Pearl bordering on St. John's.) Close to Corner Brook is the major skiing centre — not only of Newfoundland but of eastern Canada — Marble Mountain. Within an easy day's drive are the Bay of Islands and Bonne Bay. Both north and south routes of the Bay of Islands provide interesting and scenic drives while the trip around Bonne Bay offers spectacular views which cannot be matched anywhere else in the province.

Places of Interest

1. **Corner Brook.**
    1a **Glynmill Inn.** The old staff house of the Bowater Company, now a highly regarded hotel, and Corner Brook house — the mill manager's house.
    1b **Sir Wilfred Grenfell College.** The first branch of Memorial University was established in Corner Brook in 1975 (incidentally I had the privilege of being the first Principal of the College and of living in Corner Brook from 1975-77).
    1c **The James Cook Memorial.** In his early surveying expeditions Captain James Cook spent several years mapping the Newfoundland coast. He spent much time and effort char-

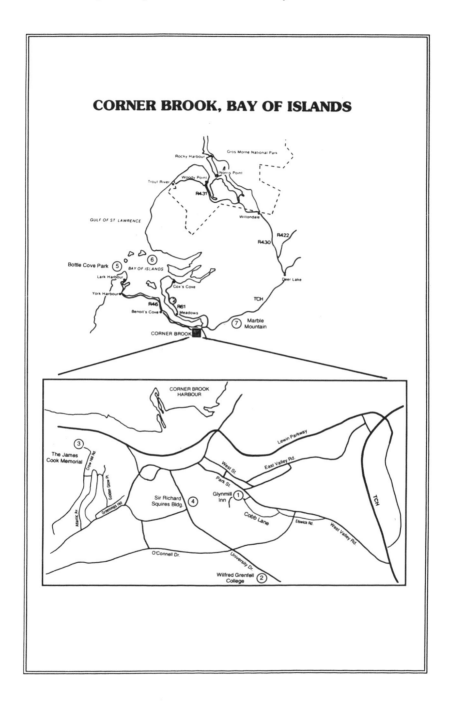

CORNER BROOK, BAY OF ISLANDS

tering the waters of the Bay of Islands, Bonne Bay and the
Northern Peninsula. The view from the Memorial is well
worth the climb.

2. **Bottle Cove Park.** An excellent provincial park. The drive
   from Corner Brook is through several picturesque communities and the picnicking opportunities are excellent.

3. **Sir Richard Squires Building** is the seat of the provincial
   government for Western Newfoundland. It is named for Sir
   Richard Squires a colourful and controversial premier of the
   province during the declining years of Responsible Government. The building is ten stories tall, the highest outside St.
   John's and in addition to government offices, houses courtrooms and a public library.

4. **The Bay of Islands.** The scenic road will take you from Lark
   Harbour on the south side to Cox's Cove on the north. The
   islands for which the bay is named are Woods Island and
   Gurnsey Tweed and Pearl. The bay is a favourite for sailboats
   and other pleasure craft.

5. **Marble Mountain** is the most active skiing centre in Eastern
   Canada. There are twenty-six runs ranging in difficulty from
   the gentle beginners slopes through those requiring more
   expert levels of skill to the stomach churning drop of OMJ (ask
   one of the locals what the initials stand for).

My Recommendations —

- The falls in the brook at the end of Cox's Cove is worth driving the extra few miles.
- Driving on the high land around Corner Brook and the Bay of Islands is a pure delight.
- When driving to Corner Brook from the east or away from the west the road takes a scenic route close to the Humber River. Try to identify the "Man in the Mountain" in the headland opposite.
- In the early fall, drive through Lady Bowater Park. It presents the most dramatic pattern of autumn colors imaginable.
- The southern shore of Bonne Bay is a scenic must. There are few communities in Newfoundland to match the beauty of Woody Point with its lombardy poplars.

Places to eat and overnight —

- The old country charm of the Glynmill Inn cannot be beaten.
- The steaks in the Wine Cellar are about the tastiest that I have encountered.
- The view from the dining room of the Mamateek Inn is spectacular and panoramic.
- Strawberry Hill, formerly a VIP retreat for Bowater executives, combines a luxurious atmosphere with marvelous scenery and near-by salmon fishing.
- Victoria Manor in Woody Point for comfort and other world charm.
- Sugar Hill in Norris Point (their menu rivals that of a five star restaurant).

The Northern Peninsula and Southern Labrador

The Northern peninsula begins where the Viking Trail (Highway No. 430) turns off at Deer Lake. The trail takes you first through the rugged scenery of the Long Range Mountains to the spectacular beauty of Bonne Bay. This area has been selected as the location for the second of Newfoundland's national parks — Gros Morne — which is far larger and more dramatic than its eastern counterpart, Terra Nova. The park itself offers magnificent scenery, an excellent interpretation center, picnic and camp sites, trails and rides. Continuing north the road is surrounded and sometimes covered with drifting white sand for a few miles. The wood north of the park is unique in the province — the tuckamore trees are almost flattened by the wind — as the ocean rolls into windswept beaches and the vegetation huddles against the force of the wind. On the right the Long Range Mountains, set back at some distance from the road, offer a continually changing vista of valleys, fiords and cloud shrouded peaks. When the road turns right after Plum Point the scenery changes dramatically, and for several miles the scattered rocks left by glaciers long ages ago give an almost lunar quality to the experience. Then the road touches the bottom of Pistolet Bay and continues on to the heart of Grenfell country, St. Anthony. North of St. Anthony you will find two treasures of early European exploration of North America — the Viking site at L'Anse aux Meadows and the Basque whaling site at Red Bay in Labrador.

Places of Particular Interest

1. **Bonne Bay.** The southern route from Wiltondale takes you through Glenterrace and Winterbrook into Woody Point, well known for its charm and its stately lombardy poplars. A side trip will take you through a dramatic rift valley to Trout River. The stark tableland mountains with its snowy tablecloth in spring and early summer present an opportunity for serious hiking. (Try the Green Gardens trail.)

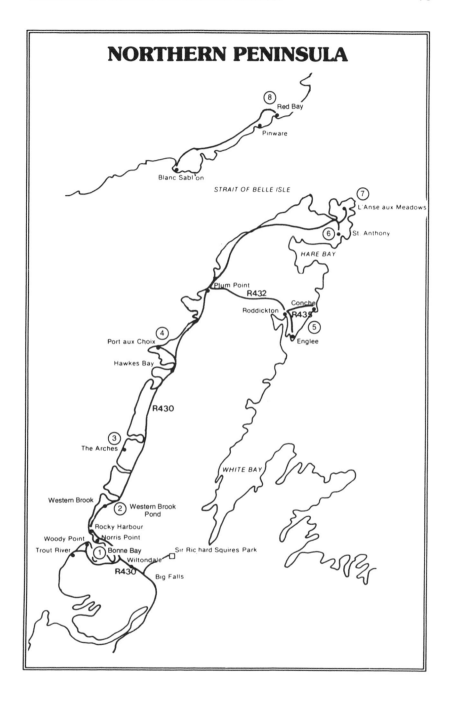

NORTHERN PENINSULA

1. **Western Brook Pond.** The mountains which make up this magnificent fiord were formed millions of years ago and were moved away from the sea when the underlying base rock tilted. The lake and the fiord itself were shaped by glacial action and now offer one of the most spectacular views in the province. A lovely trail takes you into the pond. Boat tours are available during the summer months.

2. **The Arches.** Midway between Daniel's Harbour and Portland Creek you will find a magnificent geological curiosity. Located just off the highway is a massive dolomite formation into which the action of the sea has carved two large arches. A good picnic spot.

3. **Port au Choix.** A thriving fishing settlement, especially for Gulf shrimp, the town has become well known in recent years because of the discovery of remains and relics of Archaic Indians. Today a tasteful museum presents samples of the artifacts and interesting information. An archaeological team from Memorial University is still working at the dig during the summer months.

4. **Englee, Conche, Croque.** Old fishing villages which date back to the time when the area was part of the French shore. The treaty of Utrecht gave the French permission to use certain areas of northern Newfoundland for the drying and curing of fish. Stages, wharves and flakes could be erected without fear of penalty or destruction from British warships.

5. **St. Anthony.** The base of Dr. Wilfred Grenfell's far reaching medical service to northern Newfoundland and Labrador. Dr. Grenfell first came to Newfoundland in 1892 as a doctor with Mission for Seafarers and returned to start a medical practice which provided excellent service to the entire region. Other activities of the mission included a wider range of social services and the development of a centre for the production and distribution of crafts. Promising young doctors and nurses were recruited from North America and Europe and the fame of the mission spread worldwide. Dr. Grenfell's

house has been restored and the Curtis hospital contains an interesting and attractive mural.

6. **L'Anse aux Meadows.** One thousand years ago the Vikings led by Leif Erikson came from Greenland and for some years maintained a viable settlement at L'Anse aux Meadows. They were eventually driven off by the aboriginals or Beothuks ("the skrallings") but left evidence of their stay behind them. In the early 1960s Dr. Helge Ingstead excavated the grounds which covered the site and found the outline of houses and some domestic ornaments. These were eventually authenticated as dating back to 1000 A.D. and the area became a UNESCO World Historic Site. There is an excellent information center and the original buildings may easily be identified and toured.

7. **Red Bay.** Before John Cabot came to Newfoundland, Basque whalers established whaling stations on the Labrador coast. Numerous artifacts have been found and a vessel, the *San Juan*, which sunk in a storm in the 1500s, has been found and researched. Several gravesites, each containing the bodies of several young men, have been found.

My Recommendations

- Turn off at Wiltondale and drive along the south side of Bonne Bay to Woody Point. A side trip to Trout River is well worth the time and effort.
- Visit Big Falls in Sir Richard Squires Park. The sight of the salmon leaping the falls in the second half of July and August is one of the natural wonders of the world.
- Take the James Callahan Trail (named after a British Prime Minister) to the top of Gros Morne.
- Visit the Gros Morne Interpretation Center.
- Hike into Western Brook Pond and take a boat trip to the upper end of the pond.
- Picnic at "The Arches."
- Visit the interpretation center at Port au Choix. The talks and displays are excellent.
- Take a leisurely tour of St. Anthony and see the Dr. Grenfell House.

- The Curtis Hospital has a stunning ceramic mural in its entrance foyer-it depicts major trends from the area's history.
- Visit the UNESCO historic site at L'Anse aux Meadows.
- Take the ferry from St. Barbe to Blanc Sablon and visit the excellent Basque Intrepretation Centre at Red Bay (a full day's trip from Plum Point).

Places to eat and overnight —

- Eat at Parsons Hospitality Home in Rocky Harbour. The finest home cooking and a warm atmosphere.
- Stay at either The Tickle Inn at Cape Onion-famous for its family atmosphere and its superb food — or the Valhalla Inn at Gunners Cove. Both highly recommended.
- The Sugarhill at Norris Point has an international profile for its cooking and decor, both of which are stunning.
- If you stop at the Seaview Motel in Forteau, you must have the fish chowder.
- The Dockside Inn in St. Barbe.
- The Northern Lights Inn, Lance au Clair.
- The Lighthouse Restaurant, St. Anthony.
- Eat at The Lighthouse Restaurant in St. Anthony and in June and July watch the icebergs drift past.

The motels on the Northern Peninsula (The Sea Echo in Port au Choix, The Dockside in St. Barbe, The Northern Lights in Lance au Clair and the St. Anthony in St. Anthony all provide good accommodation and food — but the Plum Point in Plum Point and the Ocean View in Rocky Harbour receive special praise for their food and service.

Newfoundland by Sea

Getting to the Island

Since Newfoundland is an island, your trip (unless of course you come by air) must include a sea voyage. In the past numerous vessels came to Newfoundland from Halifax, Boston and Montreal. Today all passenger and vehicle transportation is provided by Marine Atlantic which offers two routes to Newfoundland. The shorter and most popular is the North Sydney-Port aux Basques route. The ferries (*The Caribou* and *The Smallwood* are the largest superferries in North America) leave each port several times each day and the trip takes less than six hours. The longer route is from North Sydney to Argentia, which is less than one hour and a half to St. John's. The trip takes 14 hours, and is offered three days a week Monday, Wednesday and Friday with a 7:00 a.m. departure from North Sydney and an 11:30 p.m. departure from Argentia.

Time was when the only way that you could see the coastal communities was by sea. In the early 1900s, the Alphabet Fleet, ordered by the Reid Newfoundland Railway Company, covered all Newfoundland towns by regularly scheduled trips. In Trinity, the regular calls of the Glencoe and Kyle, and the occasional calls of the Northern Ranger on her way north, or the 'Bay Boat' the Ethie, were eagerly awaited and greeted by a full turnout of all inhabitants. Before 1911, the only way to get from Trinity to St. John's was by coastal steamer or schooner.

Then came the roads and railway. The railway, constructed in the 1890s, opened the Bonavista branch in 1911. In 1949 the Cabot Highway ran from Bonavista to St. John's, a ten hour journey over mostly dirt roads. (Today the trip takes three and a half hours.) As ground transportation, especially the highways, improved, the need for steamers and schooners declined and they eventually disappeared. Still, today there are areas of the province where sea transportation is a necessity: the islands on the northeast coast, the south coast, and the coast of Labrador.

The Labrador Coast

For a quick trip, especially if you wish to take a vehicle, the car ferry *The Robert Bond* leaves Lewisporte and steams to Goose Bay with an intermediate stop in Cartwright. This 38 hour journey takes you past the northern tip of Newfoundland, along the south Labrador coast, and then over 100 miles through Hamilton Inlet and Groswater Bay to Goose Bay.

For the more adventurous, or those with more time, Marine Atlantic offers a cruising Labrador service from the first of July until the end of October. Sailing from St. Anthony, the 12 day return trip makes many ports of call, including Red Bay, Port Hope Simpson, Makkovik and Nain. For information or reservations call (709) 695-7957, or 1-800-341-7981, or write Cruising Labrador, Marine Atlantic Inc., P.O. Box 520, Port aux Basques, Newfoundland, A0M 1C0, or fax (709) 695-4209.

The Island Ferries

These are the remaining portions of the once thriving coastal fleet which called at all the outports. More information can be obtained from the Department of Works, Services and Transportation (709) 229-7968 or from each service —

1. Bell Island — from Portugal Cove, two ferries operating from 6:45 a.m. to midnight, crossing time 20 minutes. (709) 895-3541.

2. St. Brendan's — from Burnside, one ferry, crossing time 45 minutes, request runs (3-5 per day). (709) 466-7952.

3. Change Islands — from Farewell, one ferry, frequent runs, crossing time 25 minutes. (709) 627-3492 or -4352.

4. Fogo Island — from Farewell, one ferry, crossing time 50 minutes, several times a day. (709) 627-3492 or -3448.

5. Little Bay Islands — from Shoal Arm, one ferry, crossing time 45 minutes. (709) 292-4300 or 673-4352.

6. Long Island — from Pelley's Island, one ferry, crossing time 5 minutes. (709) 292-4300 or 673-4352.

7. Harbour Deep — from Jackson's Arm, one ferry makes the three hour crossing on Tuesdays, Wednesdays, Fridays and Sundays. (709) 635-4127.

MARINE ATLANTIC ROUTES

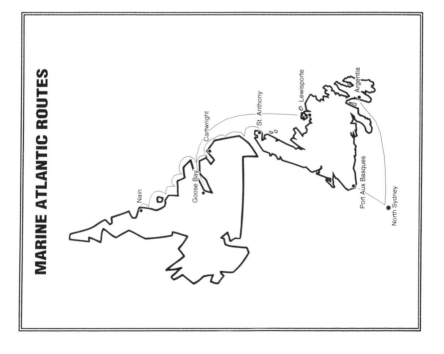

Nain

Cartwright

Goose Bay

St. Anthony

Lewisporte

Argentia

Port Aux Basques

North Sydney

INTRA-PROVINCIAL FERRY SERVICE

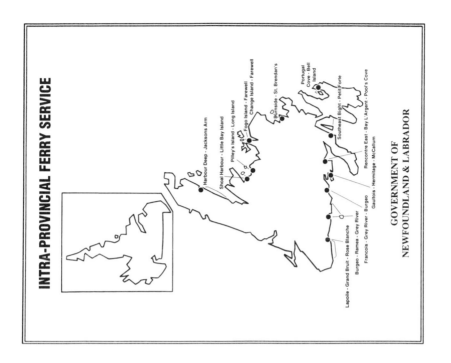

Harbour Deep - Jacksons Arm

Shoal Harbour - Little Bay Island

Pilley's Island - Long Island

Fogo Island - Farewell

Change Island - Farewell

Bonavista - St. Brendan's

Portugal Cove - Bell Island

Southeast Bight - Petit Forte

Rencontre East - Bay L'Argent - Pool's Cove

Gaultois - Hermitage - McCallum

Francois - Grey River - Burgeo

Burgeo - Ramea - Grey River

Lapoile - Grand Bruit - Rose Blanche

GOVERNMENT OF
NEWFOUNDLAND & LABRADOR

The South Coast

Until a few years ago, a CN vessel (the last of which was the Hopedale) served all the communities between Argentia and Port aux Basques. Each trip took a week, with a stop at St. Pierre. This delightful journey has unfortunately passed into history. Today, sections of the south coast still inaccessible by road or rail are served by five different ferries. On the extreme southwest, La Poile and Grand Bruit (with its charming waterfall) are served from Rose Blanch. McCallum and Gaultois are served from Hermitage. In Fortune Bay, Recontre East, Bay L'Argent and Pool's Cove are connected by a local ferry. In Placentia Bay, Petit Forte and Paradise can be reached from Argentia. The central part of the south coast, the most isolated and scenic part, are all served from Burgeo. One ferry connects Grey River and Francois and another serves Ramea and Grey River. The ferries do not provide overnight accommodation and the schedules are not synchronized so travelling the south coast can present a problem. Nevertheless the informed traveller can plan a pleasant journey. First proceed to Burgeo by road — the best time is to travel on a Tuesday and overnight in Burgeo. On Wednesday, at 2 p.m., board the Marine Voyager and sail to Grey River and Francois (travel time approximately 5 hours). Overnight in Francois in a Bed and Breakfast. Thursday, at 8 a.m., depart on the same vessel for McCallum and Hermitage (travel time approximately 4 hours). You can have your car driven from Burgeo to Hermitage. (For specific arrangements I recommend contacting Mrs. Irene Parsons in Burgeo, (709) 886-2544.) Once in Hermitage, you can take another ferry and overnight in Gaultois, or you can return to the Trans Canada Highway at Bishop's Falls. Or you can stay and explore the historic and beautiful Bay d'Espoir.

Note: Small, private companies are beginning to offer tours along the Labrador and South Coasts. **Discovery Tours** may be able to help with local contacts. Call (709) 722-4533.

The Newfoundland Language

The language spoken in Newfoundland, especially in the more remote outports, is a source of puzzlement and amusement for visitors and provides a rich vein for scholarly research for those interested in language, linguistics and folklore. Centuries of isolation have, until recently, preserved ancient meanings and long lost constructions of the language of Dorset or Devon, and of Cork and Waterford. During the past few years scholarly papers and theses, especially the highly regarded *Dictionary of Newfoundland English*, have provided interesting and entertaining insights into the "way one speaks."

For many years local amateurs have been interested in the Newfoundland use of words and some have recorded their comments. To give you a sample of some of the more common of the local expressions I present a poem penned some seventy years ago by my mother, Rose M. Sullivan.

> I'M FIRST RATE B'Y HOW'S YERSELF
> The typical Newfoundlander
> (And I'm proud that I am one)
> Besides the King's good English
> Has a language all his own;
> For instance if you meet one
> And enquire about his health—
> He's not "just fine" nor "like the bird"
> He's "First rate b'y, how's yerself".

We all know what a "grapple" is
    A "haul-off" and "killock"
I spent my time around the punts
    Although I was a "twillick".
There's "slewed around" and "went to work"
    "Turned to" and "took a spell";
While of "clever-lookin" boys and girls
    I'm sure you've all "heard tell".
We go round the "ballyca'ters"
    When there's "swatches" in the ice,
And only a Newfoundlander
    Can "fall down" and "get a h'ist."
You'd never guess a "bedlamer"
    Is an adolescent lad,
While intermittent snowflurries
    Are "dwighs" or "just a scad."
Now other people say "down South"
    This I don't understand—
For everybody always says
    "Down North" in Newfoundland
"Bide where you're at," or "leff en bide"
    You'll hear the old folks say;
And if you're drinking "switchel"
    That's black, unsweetened tea.
Some think we live on "fish and spuds"
    This fairly makes me boil,
Yet 'tis a treat when spring comes 'round
    To get a meal of "swile."
A local dish is "fish and brewis"
    The youngsters like the "scrunchions"
And they love the "lassy sugar"
    From the bottom of the "puncheons."
But times bring alteration—
    and soon we'll hear no more
Those quaint old local sayings
    As in the days of yore.

Yet in my heart I treasure them,
    They always seem to be
A precious part of Home Sweet Home
    To simple folk like me.

Glossary

Grapple (graplen) — a light metal anchor to moor small boats.

Haul-off — a rope which is passed through an underwater collar to permit a boat to be hauled off, tied at the mooring, and hauled in again.

Killock — a small boat anchor made of a wooden frame enclosing rocks.

Twillick — a young and undersized child

Clever-looking — big and good looking

Slewed — to bend, twist or turn

Ballyca'ters — ice which rests on the shore

Swatches — an area of open water or thin ice

Bide — to remain or stay put

Swile — Seal

Fish and brewis — cod fish cooked with hard tack or sea biscuits

Scrunchions — small chunks of fat pork that are fried with the fish and brewis

Lassy — molasses

Puncheons — a large barrel in which lassy (molasses) was imported. The lassy sugar collected on the bottom of the barrel and was an unusual and delightful treat.

Newfoundland Folklore

Linguistics, the specific meaning and use of words, and folklore, "the broader aspects of Newfoundland life and culture", have been of interest to amateur students for many years — under these and less academic names. As Canon George Earle has pointed out "what they call folklore now we used to call old foolishness."

The following section first appeared in *Historic Newfoundland*.

Folk Lore has been defined as race experience crystallized into story, song or saying. A visitor to Newfoundland is amused and charmed by the quaint speech of the fisherfolk and by the originality and picturesque form of their homemade phrases. The St. John's accent has a pronounced Irish quality, and the same may be said of the districts of Harbour Main, Ferryland and Placentia. In the north of the Island one hears an altogether different pronunciation, and listens to a Dorset or Devon dialect of three centuries ago with words and idioms long lost in England. More interesting than this variety of accent are the homely figures of speech that have their origin in environment through four centuries of settlement. These idioms have an unusual type of literary value because of their simplicity and their redolence of the things of Newfoundland life.

In the following pages we present a selection of Newfoundland folk lore which is classified under various headings. First we give a vocabulary of unusual words with their meanings. This is not by any means a full list, but has been culled from a collection gathered from every part of the province. Meanings and origins are given wherever possible; it is not always certain where a word originated, and its present spelling is obviously phonetic.

Next we give an interesting list of Newfoundland sayings. Some of these were brought out from England and Ireland by the early settlers. Others are of the type coined in this province, and are moulded from contacts with nature through generations of hardy toilers of the sea. These are the most valuable portion of the island's folk lore, and are indeed the very essence of race experience. These sayings are of two kinds, one taking the form of a mere peculiar expression, and the second being a homely simile or metaphor terse and picturesque.

Lastly we give a heterogeneous group of legends of multiple classifications, such as weather lore, folk medicines, omens of good or bad luck, superstitions, and quaint customs. Our sources are many, and have been derived from a lengthy study of the island's traditions. For our description of Christmas customs we owe much to the late Rev. A.C. Waghorne, the author of "The Flora of Newfoundland". We have also received invaluable aid from the writings of the late P.K. Devine, H.W. LeMessurier, and W.A. Munn.

Words and Their Meanings

amphered	infected, purulent
angishore	a weak, miserable person
anighst	near
aninst	beside
arn	any
atirt	athwart
balderdash	nonsense
bavin	wood shavings to light fires
ballyrag	to abuse
bannock	a round cake of bread
ballycater	ice formed by spray on the shore
bannikin	a small tin cup
bawn	a beach used to dry fish
barrisway	a lagoon at a rivermouth; barachoix
bass	to throw small stones
bedlamer	a seal one yer old; bete de la mer
binicky	ill-tempered
biver	to shiver with cold
blather	nonsensical talk
blear	an ignorant person
bogie	a small stove
bostoon	to complain loudly
bonnif	a young pig
brieze	to press down firmly

breach	schools of fish on the surface
brack	a crack in a dish or furniture
brishney	dry twigs gathered for fuel
brewis	hard biscuit boiled, and pork fat
bultow	a line with hooks, a trawl
calabogus	rum, molasses and spruce beer
cant	to lean to one side
chucklehead	a stupid person
chinch	to stow tightly
clink	to beat another with the fists
clamper	ice detached from berg of floe
clout	to hit an opponent hard
clum	to grapple with an adversary
clobber	an untidy state of things
covel	a covered water barrel
cotched	caught
crannicks	dried roots of trees
crossackle	to vex by contrary argument
crubeens	pickled pigs' feet
cuddy	a covered space in the bow of a boat
daddle	the hind paw of a seal
dill	a cavity in a boat from which water is bailed
doter	an old seal
douse	to give a quick blow
drung	a narrow, rocky lane
drook	a valley with steep wooded slopes
dresser	an old fashioned kitchen cupboard
drubbin	oil and tallow to preserve boots
duckish	the time between sunset and dark
duff	pudding of flour, fat pork and molasses
dulse	a kind of seaweed
dudeen	a pipe
dwoi	a short snow shower
faddle	a bundle of firewood; fardel
faggot	a pile of half-dried fish
fipper	a seal's forepaw; flipper
flankers	sparks from a chimney
flinders	small pieces

fousty	mouldy, with a bad colour
frore	frozen
frape	a rope with blocks to moor a boat
fudge	to manage daily chores alone
funk	smoke or vapour of evil odour
gansey	a woollen sweater; from Guemsey
gamogue	a silly trick
gandy	a pancake
glutch	to swallow with difficulty
glauvaun	to complain about trifles
gommil	a moron, a half fool
gruel	oatmeal porridge
grumpus	the whale
gulvin	the stomach of a codfish
gurry	blood and slime from fish
guff	impertinence
gilderoy	a proud person
gowdy	awkward
grogbits	snacks to accompany drinking
gumbeens	cubes of chewing tobacco
helf	the handle of an axe, haft
heft	to weigh in the hand
huffed	vexed
hummock	a small hill
jackeen	a rascally boy
jinker	one who brings bad luck
jut	to hit the elbow of another
kingcorn	the Adam's apple of the throat
klick	the stiffening at the back of a shoe
lashins	plenty
livyer	one who lives here - in contrast to a visitor
lob	not of much value
lolly	soft ice beginning to form in harbour
longers	rails for a fence
lourd	dark, gloomy
lops	small breaking seas
manus	to mutiny aboard ship
mauzy	misty
mundle	a wooden baton used to stir soup

mush	porridge
munch	to grind with the teeth; from "manger"
narn	none
nish	tender, easily injured
omadhaun	a foolish person
oonshick	a person of low intelligence
peeze	to leak in small bubbles
pishogue	a story generally discredited
plaumaush	soft talk, flattery
planchen	the floor; from "plancher"
prise	a lever
pritchet	a prop under the shaft of a cart
prog	food
puddock	the stomach
purchase	to get a firm grip on
quot	to crouch, squat
quid	a chew of tobacco; the cud
raines	a skeleton
ral	a disorderly fellow
rawny	very thin, bony
rames	a skeleton
rompse	to wrestle
sadogue	a fat, easy going person
scrammed	numb with cold
scrawb	to tear with the nails
scrimshank	hesitation to avoid an issue
scut	a dirty, mean person
shaugraun	a vagabond state
sharoused	nonplussed
scruff	the back of the neck
sish	ice broken into particles by surf
slob	ice newly frozen
slinge	to stay away from school or work
shooneen	a coward
shule	to move away backwards
smidge	a stain
sloo	to get out of the way
slieveen	a deceitful person

suent	smooth, graceful
snarbuckle	a hard knot; burnt to a cinder
strouters	posts at the end of a fishing stage
stunned	stupid and ignorant
squabby	soft as jelly
squish	the sound of waters exuding from boots
spile	a peg for a hole in a cask
sugawn	a rope made of twisted hay
swatch	to shoot seals in pools amid icefloes
swig	to drink from a bottle
switchel	cold tea
tacker	waxed hemp for sewing boots
tant	tall and slender, as trees and spars
talqual	the good with the bad, tails qualis
tantem	side by side
teeveen	a patch on a boot
titivate	to adorn exceedingly fine
tole	to entice with bait
trapse	to walk around unnecessarily
trunnel	a wooden peg in a plank; trenail
truck	payment for fish by merchandise
tuckamore	a low clump of trees
twig	to catch the meaning
twack	to examine goods and buy nothing
vang	fried salt pork
vamp	the sole of a stocking; to walk
vandue	a sale by auction; Vendu
wattle	a small slim fir
weasand	the throat
witlow	inflammation around a fingernail
whiting	a tree from which the rind has been removed
water horse	salt fish just washed from a vat
wop the wasp	a blow from a blunt weapon
yarkin	lines to fasten a net to a head rope
yean	giving birth to young by sheep
yarry	rising early; alert
yaffle	an armful of dried fish
yer	here
yoi	in this place

yerrin	a reef point; earing
yuck	to vomit
yap	to retort angrily

Newfoundland Sayings

As fine a man as ever broke a cake of the world's bread.
All mops and brooms.
   This refers to an untidy condition of the hair.
An honest man when there are no anchors around.
   Ironical tribute.
A fisherman is one rogue, a merchant is many.
A warm smoke is better than a cold fog.
A single line may have two hooks.
   A dual purpose.
An Irish youngster for the bow oar.
   He gets the spray over him.
A gunshot away.
   A short distance, about fifty yards.
A noggin to scrape.
   A very difficult task.
An hour by sun.
   An hour before sunset.
Come day, go day, God send Sunday.
   Applied to a lazy person.
Cape St. Mary's pays for all.
   This locality has a prolific fishery.
Done it brown.
   Overdid the thing — the allusion is to burnt bead.
Don't cut tails.
   Don't be too particular. Fish tails were cut as a mark.
Douse the killik.
   Throw the grapnel overboard.
Empty vessels loom biggest.
Fair weather to you and snow to your heels.
   Good luck on your way.
Far off cows wear long horns.
Fish in summer and fun in winter.
   Everything in its place.

Give her the long main sheet.

To go afar with no intention to return.

Go to law with the devil and hold court in hell.

The odds are all against you.

Jack is as good as his master.

The hired man is paid off when the end of the fishing season arrives, and is no longer a servant.

In a hobble about it.

Worrying about the matter.

If you lose your grapnel in the spring, you'll find it in the fall.

You will find it on your account at the merchant's store.

In a leaky punt with a broken oar, 'tis always best to hug the shore.

I'll go bail for that.

I will vouch for the truth of it.

Let no man steal your lines.

Beware of competition.

Long may your big jib draw.

A good wish for the future.

May snow is good for sore eyes.

An old legend; many say it is true.

Nofty was forty when he lost the pork.

Never be sure of anything; the man Nofty held the best trump but allowed an opponent to reach game.

Out dogs and in dieters.

Prepare for the summer fishery.

Praise the weather ... when you're ashore.

Don't celebrate your good fortune too soon.

Pigs may fly, but they are very unlikely birds.

Hope in vain.

Skin the old cow.

When cold March weather persists far into April the old cow dies of hunger.

Solomon Gosse's birthday.

This was Thursday when the usual meal was pork and cabbage and pudding, a favourite meal in Newfoundland.

The devil to pay and no pitch hot.

Unprepared for emergency. To "pay a boat" meant to put hot pitch over a seam between the planks.

There's favour in hell, if you bring your splits.
Said of currying favour through underhand methods.
Tom Long's account.
To pay what you owe and have nothing left.
'Tis not every day that Morris kills a cow.
Favourable opportunity comes but seldom.
The old dog for a hard road.
Experience easily overcomes difficulty.
White horses on the bay.
On a stormy day waves break into foam. The allusion to white horses is apparently a reference to an Irish tradition of a chieftain named O'Donahue who was drowned in a lake in Killarney on his wedding morn, and could afterwards be seen in a storm riding a white horse and preceded by maidens strewing flowers.
Wait a fair wind, and you'll get one.
Await opportunity.
When the snipe bawls, the lobster crawls.
After sunset.
You can't tell the mind of a squid.
This refers to an unreliable person. A squid can move backwards or forward.
You can get only one shot at a shell bird.
A shrewd person can be duped but once.
You are robbing Peter to pay Paul.
Needless change of useful things.
You'll do it in the long run.
Eventually you will succeed.
You are taking a rise out of me.
Your flattery is only for the purpose of making others laugh at me.
You are as deep as the grave.
Your real feelings are not easily judged from your appearance.
You are making a nice kettle of fish.
Making a mess of affairs.
You are moidering my brains.
Your noise is very disturbing.

Your tawts are too far aft.

The word "thwart", meaning a cross seat in a boat, is commonly pronounced "tawt" by Newfoundland fishermen. The expression means you are very wrong in your opinion.

You are too big for your boots.

You are assuming too much authority.

You can cut a notch in the beam.

Said when someone does the unusual.

You are like a fish out of water.

Not at home in your environment.

The older the crab, the tougher his claws.

It is not easy to fool a sophisticated person.

Weather Lore

Here again we find the result of race experience. The Newfoundland fisherman has to pursue his vocation in wind and sea, and generations of wisdom for forecasting storms have been handed down to him through the centuries. He has to foretell from nature just when favourable opportunity will present itself so that ventures to fishing ledges far from shore may be made with impunity. Also he has to predict rain so that fish may be spread when long periods of sunshine are practically certain. He knows the winds and ocean currents that offer the best conditions for a good catch, and he is familiar in his own way with the humidity of the atmosphere that is an adverse factor in the drying process. Below we give some of the more common signs of good and bad weather as long observed and religiously depended upon:

A red dawn is a sign of rain and storm.

A red sunset is a sign of fine weather.

Brilliant Northern Lights foretell a fine day and then storm.

Hoar frost in autumn is a sign of south wind and rain.

When gulls fly high, stormy weather may be expected.

When goats come home from the hills, expect rain soon.

When distant hills appear near, rainy weather is coming.

Rote from the shore on a calm night indicated wind from that direction the following day.

When wild animals take on thick coats of fur in autumn, it is a sign of a severe winter.

After the sun crosses the line in September, watch the wind and
   weather for the following days. Each day is said to forecast the
   weather for the individual months ahead.
When the wind shifts against the sun, Trust it not for back 'twill
   run.
When the wind is in the east, 'Tis neither good for man nor beast.
Mackerel sky and mares' tails
Make the sailor furl his sails.
Watch the new moon. If you can hang a powder horn on the lower
   rim of the crescent, it is a sign of stormy weather.
The following are common signs of rain:
Soot falling to the ground, dogs sleeping through the day, spiders
   very active, rheumatic pains with elderly people.
To dream of horses is a sign with sailormen that storms will come.
When cats are very playful, they are said to "gale up the weather".

Folk Medicines

While some of Newfoundland folk medicines do not fall into the
category of superstition, others definitely belong to the witch
doctor domain. Their origins are diverse, and we can trace customs
from continental Europe, England, Ireland, Scotland and the
Channel Islands, and from Indian and Eskimo sources on this side
of the Atlantic. Some oldtime remedies in which the use of herbs
and balsams hold primary place indicate racial knowledge of
medicinal properties. Others to which we call attention suggest
that it may be worthwhile to explore their possibilities. In the latter
class we may mention the use of alder buds and bark, the so-called
"fish doctor," the use of maggots in the Eskimo poultice, and the
curative properties of sea shells. We append some common remedies as practised in Newfoundland:
Stopping Blood — The application of cobwebs, also turpentine of
   fir. Nose bleed could be stopped by certain persons who
   recited a secret prayer or rite to achieve the desired effect.
Curing Warts — Cut notches in a stick and hide the latter. Rub a
   piece of fresh meat to the wart, then bury the meat and as it
   decayed the warts disappeared. Count the warts and make a
   like number of chalk marks on the back of a stove; as these
   burnt off the warts went also.

Toothache — Vinegar left in the mouth gave relief. Pebbles from the grave of a pious person provided a faith cure. The magician charmed away the toothache. One way to do this was to write some words on a scrap of paper and have the afflicted one carry the script on his person, but he was forbidden to read it as the pain returned in punishment of such curiosity.

Hiccoughs — Distract the attention of the sufferer momentarily.

Pain in the Side — Put a pebble under the tongue.

Headache — Walk backwards, around in circle preferably.

Boils — A poultice of soap, flour and molasses on brown paper. To extract the core of a boil, put hot water in a bottle. Then empty the bottle and place its mouth on the boil; as the bottle cooled the core came out.

Infected Sores — Many people of Newfoundland recall some old resident of their community who was regarded as remarkable in healing festered sores. It was generally some motherly old lady who did the doctoring. Scorched linen, burnt cream, white of an egg, powdered dust of sea shells, dried alder buds mixed with tar, dried and powdered seaweed, goose grease, mouldy bread — these are some of the ingredients of a good poultice.

Hernia — An old custom in order to cure a child of hernia was to split a green witch hazel tree and pass the child through it.

Stomach Trouble — The ground juniper boiled was supposed to be a panacea for stomach ills. Dogberry extract was also favourably regarded. Alder buds were also boiled and the extract used to good effect.

Haemorrhoids — Pine tar applied to the affected part produced relief.

Sore Eyes — May snow was gathered and bottled for a remedy. Many old people testify to the efficiency of this strange cure.

Incretions — Burnt ash of tobacco, powdered resin. Still used and approved by Newfoundland fisherfolk.

Nightmare — Locally known as the 'old hag.' Call the person's name backwards.

Ingrowing Nails — Drop hot tallow from a lighted candle into the part affected, and instant relief was afforded.

Rheumatism — The great brown jellyfish was bottled, and when dissolved into fluid was rubbed to the affected parts and acted as a counter irritant. One objection to this cure was the offensive odour. The magician came to the rescue with an amulet of haddock fin which, worn on the neck, was a charm against rheumatic tendencies.

Cough — The most effective home remedies were extract of wild cherry and spirits of turpentine. Kerosene oil mixed with molasses proved effective. Snake root was also steeped for a cough medicine.

Omens

Good Luck — Seeing the new moon first over the left shoulder, picking up a horseshoe on the road, picking a four leaf clover, seeing two black crows flying overhead, putting on a garment inside out by mistake, picking up a coin, picking up a pin or a white button, a rooster crowing on the doorstep, to see a baby smiling in its sleep, to dream of one's father, a bee coming into the room.

Bad Luck — Breaking a mirror, having thirteen persons at a table, coiling a rope against the sun, walking under a ladder, purchasing a broom in May, meeting a red haired woman, looking over another's shoulder into a mirror, coming in by one door and going out by another, meeting a cross-eyed person, to have a black cat cross your path, to spill salt, to cross knives on a table, to leave a knife turned blade upwards, to have a lone black crow fly over your head, to be called back just as you have begun a journey, to whistle on the water, to drop the ring at a marriage ceremony.

Death Tokens — A dog moaning near a house, a dog burying some object near one's home, a bird coming into a room, a clock which had been stopped for years suddenly striking the hours, a window blind falling without any apparent cause, a wall picture suddenly falling. When "rigor mortis" does not appear in a corpse it means that another member of the family will soon die. To dream of a wedding is a sign of a funeral. The banshee, a weird crying at night, is said to precede the death of certain persons of Irish descent in Newfoundland.

Tokens Good and Ill — A cat washing her face, sparks from a wood stove flying to the floor, a knife or fork falling, were regarded as tokens of a visit by a stranger. The first member of the assembled company at which the cat glared would be the first to die. Ringing in the ears betokened news, the right ear for good and the left for ill. To say things backwards betokened the sight of a long absent friend. It was considered taboo to step over a child, as this would stop the growth of the youngster. If a person had a cold spasm, it was said that someone was walking over the grave of the individual. It was considered very unlucky to incur the wrath of a widow, as her curse was sure to bring evil. An odd method bringing ill fortune to an enemy was to throw the dust of one's shoes over the left shoulder in that person's direction. If things went badly on Monday, it was a sure sign of a bad week.

Quaint Beliefs and Practices

Maidens sought the name of their future husbands on the eve of Midsummer. They broke an egg and kept it in a glass, and spilled it on the road next morning. The first man to walk over the egg had the same Christian name as the husband-to-be. Belief in fairies was general; old folk still persist in vouching that they have seen these little fellows dancing on the grass on moonlit nights. Children lost in the woods were said to have been led astray by fairies; as a safeguard against this, every person carried a cake of hard biscuit in a pocket. Jack o'the Lantern can still be seen on marshlands on calm nights; many believe that an evil spirit seeks to lure the unwary traveller astray. Fishermen's superstitions in boatbuilding are interesting. It was deemed necessary to have witch hazel in some part of the new craft. She was first turned with the sun, and it was lucky to have an old sail on her at the launching. Dead dogs were buried under fruit trees to ensure a good harvest. Sick calves had a peculiar knot tied over them; it was known as the worm knot. It was tied nine times and pulled clear; if it became tangled, the calf was certain to die.

Perhaps no part of the world is more productive of ghost stories than the island of Newfoundland. There we find in all their grim detail, handed down and enlarged from generation to generation, legends of the supernatural. They run the full gamut in the scale of horrors, from the ghost in the dark lane to the spectre who guards the pirate hoard and the phantom ships that appear with spectral crews. The church apparition, the graveyard with its walking dead, the cries of anguish from dark gulches where sailors went to their doom, the eerie light beyond the harbour bar, the shrieking hag beside the dark waterfall, the great black dog that emits fire from eyes and mouth, and shapeless creeping things in haunted houses with their nameless noises - all these and more the folk describe with bated breath and awesome tones. No doubt, imagination and exaggeration play a great part in these ghostly experiences and in their repeated recital. The phantom ship may be but a mirage, and St. Elmo's fire may be explained by natural causes, but the lure of the bizarre and supernatural can lead to things strange and startling.

Festal Customs

The feast of Christmas is celebrated in the Tenth Province in the good old fashioned way. Many Yuletide practices that were brought from Europe over three centuries ago are still found in Newfoundland. The custom of hauling the Yule Log through the village on Christmas Eve has disappeared but the time honoured practice of dressing as mummers is still in vogue even in the city of St. John's. One ancient rite that was popular a century ago in many outports was the performance of a play known as St. George and the dragon. A peculiar and pleasing practice still observed is the visit of young people to the baptismal sponsors on New Year's Day, to receive the latters' blessing and to partake of the traditional cakes and candy. Another ancient custom still carried on in the outports is the game of rounders. The ball is the bladder of a pig, encased in hairy bull hide, and a heavy club is used to propel the sphere to distant spaces. The game is played on the frozen surface of a lake if the ice is of sufficient strength, otherwise a level field is chosen as the scene of combat. This ancient game is regarded as the origin of the modern American baseball.

Other festal occasions are celebrated with gusto. On the night of November 5th huge bonfires are lit in every village to perpetuate Guy Fawkes' attempt to blow up the parliament buildings in the time of James I. Green boughs and tar barrels are used to create a thick smoke screen, and through this dense pall of smoke young people dance and collide with shouts of laughter. Should a novice come in good clothes, he or she is marked for a lavish smearing of burnt embers. Other times of much merriment are Pancake Night, the eve of Lent, and the feast of St. Patrick. Old time dances are all in order on these occasions, and the music of the fiddle or the inevitable accordion gives the gay throng the necessary accompaniment. One glad interlude is the singing of some folk songs by some virtuoso or the dancing of a hornpipe by a professional heel and toe artist.

Place names

Newfoundland has, perhaps, the most unusual collection of place names of any country in the world. The hackneyed manner by which other New World settlers identified their communities and natural landmarks did not appeal to the rugged types who settled here. Early day Newfoundlanders were, obviously, men of imagination and wit who were at their best when leaving place names to posterity.

Consider their humorous side. There must have been a twinkle in many an eye when such gems as these were bestowed:

Jerry's Nose	Right-in-the-Run Island
Nick's Nose Cove	Bleak Joke Cove
Come-by-Chance	Calves Nose
Blow-me-down	Nancy Oh
Lushes Bight	Little Hooping Harbour
Bumble Bee Bight	Snake's Bight
Ha Ha Bay	and, of course,
Run-by-guess	Joe Batt's Arm.

On the other hand, it is not at all difficult to appreciate the depths of despair of those who experienced hardship or disaster on the rugged coastline. They gave to us such place names as:

Gripe Point	Famish Gut
Bad Bay	Savage Cove
Bleak Island	Confusion Bay
Misery Point	Wreck Cove
Famine Point	Bareneed
Wild Bight	and there's
Breakheart Point	Empty Basket.

Then there were the happy contented settlers, whose satisfaction is reflected in such classics as —

Heart's Desire	Sweet Bay
Heart's Content	Too Good Arm
Safe Harbour	Little Paradise
Heart's Delight	Harbour Grace
Comfort Cove	Angel's Cove, and
Little Heart's Ease	Cupids.

Although there are no Londons, Parises or Birminghams in Newfoundland, there are place names which reflect the varied origins of the adventurers, colonists, soldiers, and traders who played a part in the Island's development —

English Harbour	Frenchman's Cove
Portugal Cove	Jersey Harbour
Harbour Breton	Canada Bay, and
Turk's Island	Ireland's Eye.

The French who colonized a part of the Island and, later, held fishing rights for centuries, left a host of place names, some of which have lasted through years of mispronunciation by settlers of British origin:

Bay D'Espoir (locally called and sometimes written Bay Despair).

Francois	Beaubois
Bay de Vieux	L'anse a l'Eau
Chaleur Bay	and
Cinq Cerf Bay	La Hune.

Were the early settlers good housekeepers? They may have been, if the following place names have significance —

Plate Cove	Sugar Loaf
Grate's Cove	Cape Onion
Ladle Cove	Turnip Cove
Spout Cove	Mutton Bay
Chimney Cove	Broom Point
Table Cove	Boughfig Point
Spoon Cove	Bacon Cove
Rooms	Baker's Cove

Bread Island   Cook's Harbour,
Cheese Island   and
Butter Cove   Traytown.
Tea Cove

Apparently no one was colour-blind in those far off days. At least there are many "colourful" place names —

Black Island   Orange Bay
Red Island   Blue Cove
Green Island   Dark Cove and
White Bay   Grey Islands.

Geometricians of the day had their say with —

Pyramid Point   Triangle Point and
Square Islands   Round Harbour.

The animal world gets more than its fair share of mention in:

Lion's Den   Seal's Nest Island
Bear's Cove   Boar point
Horse Chops (!)   Otter Point
Hare's Ears Point   Dragon Bay
Cow Head   Fox Roost
Dog Cove   Muskrat Brook,
Cat Gut   and
Little Cat Arm   Goat Island.

Bird life, too, has contributed a number of place names —

Pigeon Island   Goose Bay
Penguin Island   Gander Bay
Turr Island   Swan Island,
Black Duck   and
Gull Island   Eagle Island.

Of course, the fishermen who formed the bulk of early settlers could be depended upon to name —

Caplin Cove   Schooner Island
Trout River   Spudgels Cove
Fishing Ship's Harbour   Rope Cove
Herring Neck   Salmon Cove
Dog Fish Point   Ship Cove

Boat Harbour   and
Steering Island   Mooring Cove.

For the unimpressed (to this time) we may list —
Button Island
Shoe Cove
Stocking Harbour and
Petticoat Island.

Surprising as it may seem, the map shows —
Doctor's Harbour
Hatchet Cove
Sitdown Pond and Goblin.
There's a False Cape and a Mistaken Point.

Religious feeling (or lack of it) probably accounts for place
names such as —
God Bay   Devil Cove and
Sacred Bay   Nick's Nose Cove.

When all emotions and all imagination failed, even then early
Newfoundlanders rose to the occasion. What better terms could be
found than —
Nameless Cove and Harbour Harbour.

It is, of course, impossible to list all the unusual place names in
Newfoundland in a publication of this type. There are literally
thousands of other names which are just as attractive (and some
even more unusual) as those contained here. Many are in local
usage only and cannot be found on any existing map.

The origin of many Newfoundland place names is a fascinating study in itself, and, at some time or other, nearly all her
historians have devoted considerable time and research in an
endeavour to explain just some of them.

Whether interest is academic or merely casual, however, the
unique quality of our Provincial place names must fire the imagination of everyone, resident or visitor.

Folk Songs

Many old folk songs were brought to Newfoundland from England, Ireland and Scotland during more than three centuries of colonial growth. Apart from these there is another group that had its origin in the colonies on this side of the Atlantic, and there is a third aggregation that belongs solely to Newfoundland.

It is but a natural consequence that folk songs composed in Newfoundland should have as their main theme the experience of a race that has wrested its livelihood from the sea. Occasionally there are instances of other phases of life with these isolated people. There are love affairs, the eternal triangle, and the sense of loss by some lovelorn man or maiden. There are humorous situations, portrayed in a style all Newfoundland's own. There are even lullaby songs, composed from race experience and still crooned around the baby's cot. Much history has been written in songs that tell of outstanding events, of depression and failure of fisheries, and of the political animosities of party government. Many local sea shanties are parodies on the traditional British originals.

From the standpoint of literature it is rather difficult to evaluate Newfoundland folk songs. There is a certain amount of originality, and this is particularly true of the humorous songs of the John Burke type. In fact, it is difficult to find anywhere the prototype of Burke, as he most certainly touched the master key to success, the happy faculty of writing about something that nobody had previously attempted and of writing in a style altogether new. H. LeMessurier did not write many folk songs, but he immortalized "The Girl from Toslow". In our own day Scammel was inspired when he gave to the sons of Newfoundland for all time the rollicking rhyme of "The Squid Jiggin' Ground". There is simplicity in the Newfoundland folk songs, the simple stories of life, from out of the hearts of a kindly people. They are the creations of the soul of the race, and reveal the ethnic, aesthetic and historical background of an insular character.

The songs and airs published in this booklet were obtained through the kind co-operation of the late Gerald S. Doyle, O.B.E. Mr. Doyle was keenly interested in the folk songs of Newfoundland and made a lifetime hobby of collecting them. He published no less than three booklets which were distributed free of charge.

Shortly before his death, permission was given to reproduce here
the following songs, from the 1955 edition of "Old Time Songs of
Newfoundland."

Ode to Newfoundland
When Sunrays crown thy pine-clad hills,
And Summer spreads her hand,
When silvern voices tune thy rills,
We love thee smiling land,
We love thee, we love thee
We love thee, smiling land.

When blinding storm gusts fret thy shore,
And wild waves lash thy strand,
Thro' spindrift swirl and tempest roar,
We love thee wind-swept land,
We love thee, we love thee,
We love thee, wind-swept land.

When spread thy cloak of shimm'ring white
At Winter's stern command,
Thro' shortened day and starlit night,
We love thee, frozen land,
We love thee, we love thee,
We love thee, frozen land.

As loved our fathers, so we love,
Where once they stood we stand,
Their prayer we raise to heav'n above,
God guard thee, Newfoundland
God guard thee, God guard thee,
God guard thee, Newfoundland.

—*Sir Cavendish Boyle.*

I'se the B'y

I'se the b'y that builds the boat,
And I'se the b'y that sails her!
I'se the b'y that catches the fish,
And takes 'em home to Lizer.

Chorus
Hip yer partner, Sally Tibbo!
Hip yer partner, Sally Brown!
Fogo, Twillingate, Mor'ton's Harbour,
All around the circle!

Sods and rinds to cover yer flake,
Cake and tea for supper,
Codfish in the spring o' the year,
Fried in maggoty butter.

I don't want your maggoty fish,
That's no good for winter;
I could buy as good as that
Down in Bonavista.

I took Lizer to a dance,
And faith, but she could travel'
And every step that she did take
Was up to her knees in gravel.

A Great Big Sea Hove in Long Beach

A great big sea hove in Long Beach
Right fol-or-al Ta-deedle, I do;
A great big sea hove in Long Beach
And Granny Snooks she lost her speech,
To my right fol didy fol dee.

A great big sea hove in the Harbour,
Right fol-or-al Ta-deedle, I do;
A great big sea hove in the Harbour,
And hove right up in Keough's Parlour,
To me right fol didy fol dee.

Oh dear mother I wants a sack,
Right fol-or-al Ta-deedle, I do;
Oh dear mother I wants a sack
With beads and buttons All down the back,
To me right fol didy fol dee.

Me boot is broke, me frock is tore,
Right fol-or-al Ta-deedle, I do;
Me boot is broke, me frock is tore,
But Georgie Snooks I do adore,
To me right fol didy fol dee.

Oh fish is low and flour is high.
Right fol-or-al Ta-deedle, I do
Fish is low and flour is high,
So Georgie Snooks he can't have I,
To me right fol didy fol dee.

But he will have me in the Fall,
Right fol-or-al Ta-deedle, I do;
If he don't I'll hoisy my sail
And say good-bye to old Cannaille,
To me right fol didy fol dee.

Squid-Jiggin' Ground

Oh! this is the place where the fishermen gather,
With oil skins and boots and Cape-Anns battened down,
All sizes of figures with squid lines and jiggers,
They congregate here on the squid jiggin' ground.

Some are workin' their jiggers while others are yarnin',
There's some standin' up and some more lyin' down,
While all kinds of fun, jokes and tricks are begun
As they wait for the squid on the squid-jiggin' ground.

There's men of all ages and boys in the bargain,
There's old Billy Chafe and there's young Raymond Brown;
Right younder is "Bobby" and with him is "Nobby",
They're a-chawin' hard tack on the squid-jiggin' ground.

There's men from the Harbour and men from the Tickle,
In all kinds of motor boats, green, gray and brown;
There's red-headed Tory out here in a dory,
a runnin' down Squires on the squid-jiggin' ground.

The man with the whiskers is old Jacob Steele;
He's gettin' well up but he's still pretty sound;
While Uncle Bob Hawkins wears three pairs of stockin's
Whenever he's out on the squid-jiggin' ground.

God bless my sou-wester there's Skipper John Chaffey.
He's the best man at squid-jiggin' here, I'll be bound.
Hello! What's the row? Why, he jiggin' one now—
The very first squid on the squid-jiggin' ground.

There's poor Uncle Billy, his whiskers are spattered
With spots of the squid juice that's flyin' around.
One poor little boy got it right in the eye
But they don't care a hang on the squid-jiggin ground.

Holy smoke! What a bussel; all hands are excited.
It's a wonder to me that nobody is drowned.
There's a bussel, confusion, a wonderful hussel;
They're all jiggin' squid on the squid jigging ground.

Says Bobby: "The squid are on top of the water
I just got me jigger about one fanthom down"—
When a squid in the boat squirted right down his throat
And he's swearin' like made on the squid-jiggin' ground.

Now if you ever feel inclined to go squiddin'
Leave your white shirt and collars behind in the town,
And if you get cranky without a silk hanky
You'd better steer clear of the squid-jiggin' ground.

   — *A.R. Scammel.*

Let Me Fish Off Cape St. Mary's

Take me back to my Western boat,
Let me fish off Cape St. Mary's
Where the hog downs sail and the fog horns wail
With my friends the Browns and the Cleary's.
Let me fish off Cape St. Mary's.

Let me feel my dory lift
To the broad Atlantic combers,
Where the tide rips swirl and the wild ducks whirl
Where Old Neptune calls the numbers
'Neath the broad Atlantic combers...

Let me sail up Golden Bay
With my oilskins all a'streamin'...
From the thunder squall — when I hauled me trawl
And my old Cape Ann a gleamin'
With my oil skins all a'streamin'...

Let me view that rugged shore,
Where the beach is all aglisten
With the caplin spawn where from dusk to dawn
You bait your trawl and listen
To the undertow a-hissin'.

When I reach that last big shoal
Where the ground swells break asunder,
Where the wild sands roll to the surges toll.
Let me be a man and take it
When my dory fails to make it.

Take me back to the snug Green Cove
Where the seas roll up their thunder.
There let me rest in the earth's cool Breast
Where the stars shine out their wonder
And the seas roll up their thunder.

             —*Otto P. Kelland.*

Feller from Fortune

Oh,— there's lots of fish in Bonavist Harbour,
Lots of fish right in around here;
Boys and girls are fishin' together,
Forty-five from Carbonear,

Oh,— catch-a-hold this one, catch-a-hold that one,
Swing around this one, swing around she;
Dance around this one, dance around that one,
Diddle dum this one, diddle dum-dee.

Oh,— Sally goes to church ev'ry Sunday
Not to sing nor for to hear;
But to see the Feller from Fortune,
What was down here fishin' the year.

Oh,— Sally got a bouncin' new baby,
Father said that he didn't care;
Because he like the Feller from Fortune,
What was down here fishin' last year.

Oh,— there's lots of fish in Bonavista Harbour,
Lots of fish right in around here;
Boys and girls are fishin' together,
Forty-five from Carbonear.

The Kelligrew's Soiree

You may talk of Clara Nolan's ball,
Or anything you choose,
But it couldn't hold a snuffbox
To the spree at Kelligrew's.
If you want your eyeballs straightened,
Just come out new week with me
And you'll have to wear your glasses
At the Kelligrew's Soiree.

Chorus

There was birch rine, tar twine,
Cherry wine and turpentine,
Jowls and cavalances, ginger beer and tea,—
Pig's feet, cat's meat, dumplings boiled in a sheet,
Dandelion and crackies' teeth
At the Kelligrew's Soiree.

Oh, I borrowed Cluney's beaver,
As I squared my yards to sail;
And a swallow-tail from Hogan
That was foxy on the tail;
Billy Cuddahie's old working pants
And Patsy Nolan's shoes,
And an old white vest from Fogarty
To sport at Kelligrew's

Chorus

There was Dan Milley, Joe Lily,
Tantan and Mrs. Tilley,
Dancing like a little filly;
'Twould raise your heart to see.
Jim Brine, Din Ryan, Flipper Smith and Caroline;
I tell you boys, we had a time
At the Kelligrew's Soiree.

Oh, when I arrived at Betsy Snooks'
That night at half past eight,
the place was blocked with carriages
Stood waiting at the gate,
With Cluney's funeral on my pate.
The first words Betsy said:
"Here comes a local preacher
With the pulpit on his head."

Chorus

There was Bill Mews, Dan Hughes,
Wilson, Taft, and Teddy Roose,
While Bryant he sat in the blues
And looking hard at me;

Jim Fling, Tom King,
And Johnson, champion of the ring,
And all the boxers I could bring,
At the Kelligrew's Soiree.

The Saritoga Lancers first,
Miss Betsy kindly said;
Sure I danced with Nancy Cronan
And her Grannie on the "Head";
And Hogan danced with Betsey,
Oh, you should have seen his shoes,
As he lashed old muskets from the rack
That night at Kelligrews.

Chorus

There was boiled guineas, cold guineas,
Bullocks; heads and picaninies,
And everything to catch the pennies,
You'd break your sides to see;
Boiled duff, cold duff, apple jam was in a cuff;
I tell you, boys, we had enough
At the Kelligrew's Soiree.

Crooked Flavin struck the fiddler
And a hand I then took in;
You should see George Cluney's beaver,
And it flattened to the rim!
And Hogan's coat was like a vest—
The tails were gone you see,
Oh, says I "the devil haul ye
And your Kelligrew's Soiree."

—*John Burke*

Star of Logy Bay

Ye ladies and ye gentlemen,
I pray you lend an ear
While I locate the residence of a lovely charmer fair.
The curling of her yellow locks
First stole my heart away
And her place of habitation
Is down in Logy Bay.

It was on a summer's evening
This little place I found.
I met her aged father,
Who did me sore confound;
Saying: "If you address my daughter,
I'll send her far away,
And she never will return again
While you're in Logy Bay."

How could you be so cruel as
to part me from my love?
Her tender heart heats in her breast
As constant as a dove.
Oh, Venus was no fairer,
Nor the lovely month of May,
May heaven above shower down its love
On the Star of Logy Bay.

'Twas on the very next morning
He went to St. John's town
And engaged for her a passage
In a vessel outward bound.
He robbed me of my heart's delight,
And sent her far away;
And left me here downhearted
For the star of Logy Bay.

Oh, now I'll go a-roaming;
I can no longer stay.
I'll search the wide world over
In every country.
I'll search in vain thro' France and Spain,
Likewise America
'Til I will sight my heart's delight
The Star of Logy Bay.

Tickle Cove Pond

In cuttin' and haulin' in frost and in snow
We're up against troubles that few people know
And only by patience with courage and grit
And eatin' plain food can we keep ourselves fit.
The hard and the aisey we take as it comes.
And when ponds freeze over we shorten our runs,
To hurry my hauling the Spring coming on.
Near lost me my mare on Tickle Cove Pond.

Chorus
Oh, lay hold William Oldford, lay hold William White,
Lay hold of the cordage and pull all your might,
Lay hold of the bowline and pull all you can,
And give me a lift for poor Kit on the pond.

I knew that the ice became weaker each day,
But still took the risk and kept hauling away,
One evening in April, bound home with a load.
The mare showed some halting against the ice road
and knew more than I did, as matters turned out,
And lucky for me had I joined in her doubt.
She turned 'round her head, and with tears in her eyes,
As if she were saying, "You're risking our lives."

Repeat Chorus

All this I ignored with a whip-handle blow,
For man is too stupid dumb creatures to know
The very next minute the pond gave a sigh,
And down to our necks went poor Kitty and I.

For if I had taken wise Kitty's advice
I never would take the short cut on the ice
"Poor creature she's dead and poor creature she's gone;
I'll never get my wood off Tickle Cove Pond."

Repeat Chorus

I raised an alarm you could hear for a mile
And neighbours turned up in a very short while
You can always rely on the Oldfords and Whites
to render assistance in all your bad plights.
To help a poor neighbour is part of their lives;
the same I can say of their children and wives.
When the bowline was fastened around the mare's breast
William White for a shanty song made a request.

Repeat Chorus

There was no time for thinking, no time for delay,
So straight from his head came this song right away;
"Lay hold William Oldford, lay hold William White,
Lay hold of the hawser and pull all your might,
Lay hold to the bowline and pull all you can"
And with that we brought Kit out of Tickle Cove Pond.

Repeat Chorus

Ryans and the Pittmans

We'll rant and we'll roar like true Newfoundlanders
We'll rant and we'll roar on deck and below
Until we see bottom inside the two sunkers
When straight through the channel to Toslow we'll go.

I'm a son of a sea-cook, and a cook in a trader;
I can dance, I can sing, I can reef the mainboom,
I can handle a jigger, and cuts a big figure
Whenever I gets in a boat's standing room.

If the voyage is good, then this fall I will do it;
I wants two pound ten for a ring and the priest,
A couple o'dollars for clane shirt and collars,
And a handful o'coppers to make up a feast.

There's plump little Polly, her name is Goldsworthy;
There's John Coady's Kitty, and Mary Tibbo;
There's Clara from Bruley, and young Martha Foley,
But the nicest of all is my girl in Toslow.

Farewell and adieu to ye fair ones of Valen,
Farewell and adieu to ye girls in the Cove;
I'm bound to the Westward, to the wall with the hole in,
I'll take her from Toslow the wide world to rove.

Farewell and adieu to ye girls of St. Kyran's,
Of Paradise and Presque, Big and Little Bona,
I'm bound unto Toslow to marry sweet Biddy.
And if I don't do so, I'm afraid of her da.

I've bought me a house from Katherine Davis,
A twenty-pound bed from Jimmy McGrath;
I'll get me a settle, a pot and a kettle;
Then I'll be ready for Biddy — Hurrah!

I went to a dance one night at Fox Harbour;
There were plenty of girls, so nice as you'd wish,
There was one pretty maiden achawing of frankgum,
Just like a young kitten a-gnawing fresh fish.

Then here is a health to the girls of Fox Harbour,
Of Oderin and Presque, Crabbes Hole and Bruley.
Now let ye be jolly, don't be melancholy.
I can't marry all, or in chokey I'd be.

Jack Was Every Inch A Sailor

Now 'twas twenty five or thirty years since Jack first saw the light.
He came into this world of woe one dark and stormy night.
He was born on board his father's ship as she was lying
to 'bout twenty five or thirty miles southeast of Bacalieu.

Chorus
Jack was ev'ry inch a sailor,
Five and twenty years a whaler,
Jack was ev'ry inch a sailor,
He was born upon the bright blue sea.

When Jack grew up to be a man, he went to the Labrador.
He fished in Indian Harbour, where his father fished before.
On his returning in the fog, he met a heavy gale,
And Jack was swept into the sea and swallowed by a whale.

Repeat Chorus

The whale went straight for Baffin's Bay, about ninety knots an
    hour.
And every time he'd blow a spray he'd sind it in a shower.
"O, now," says Jack unto himself, "I must see what he's about."
He caught the whale all by the tail and turned him inside out.

Repeat Chorus

For further information —

The Department of Tourism, Culture and Recreation provides comprehensive information services to tourists. The annual *Travel Guide* includes detailed and interesting information on attractions, events and accommodation for all areas of the province.

The tourist information offices carry local brochures and publications.

The Department also offers a free information service which is available inside and outside the province by calling

1-800-563-NFLD

In St. John's visit the Tourist Information offices in City Hall or on the Waterfront.

Information concerning Bed and Breakfast accommodation may be obtained from *The Annual Guide to Bed & Breakfast Hospitality Homes and Country Inns, Association of Newfoundland and Labrador*, P.O. Box 206, Gander, Newfoundland, A1V 1W6, Telephone (709) 256-4770, or Fax (709) 256-4551.

The publication *Food and Entertainment in St. John's* can be obtained from 8A Forest Road, St. John's, NF, A1C 2B9, Telephone (709) 754-0610.

Arthur M. Sullivan was born in Trinity, Trinity Bay and received his early education there and at St. Bons. He graduated from Memorial, Dalhousie, McGill and Oxford Universities. For thirty-three years he was a faculty member of Memorial University and served in various senior academic positions. His work as Director of Extension for Memorial University and as Chief Commissioner of the Commission of Inquiry into Newfoundland Transportation took him to virtually every community in the Province. In recent years he has become active as tour organizer and guide and has recently formed Discovery Tourist Services, Inc.